AUSTEN'S *EMMA*

Continuum *Reader's Guides*

Continuum's *Reader's Guides* are clear, concise and accessible introductions to classic literary texts. Each book explores the themes, context, criticism and influence of key works, providing a practical introduction to close reading and guiding the reader towards a thorough understanding of the text. Ideal for undergraduate students, the guides provide an essential resource for anyone who needs to get to grips with a literary text.

Achebe's *Things Fall Apart* – Ode Ogede
Chaucer's *The Canterbury Tales* – Gail Ashton
Conrad's *Heart of Darkness* – Allan Simmons
Dickens's *Great Expectations* – Ian Brinton
Eliot's *Middlemarch* – Josie Billington
Fitzgerald's *The Great Gatsby* – Nicolas Tredell
Fowles's *The French Lieutenant's Woman* – William Stephenson
Salinger's *The Catcher in the Rye* – Sarah Graham
William Blake's *Poetry* – Jonathan Roberts

AUSTEN'S *EMMA*

GREGG A. HECIMOVICH

continuum

Continuum International Publishing Group
The Tower Building   80 Maiden Lane
11 York Road   Suite 704
London SE1 7NX   New York, NY 10038

www.continuumbooks.com

British Library Cataloguing-in-Publication Data
A catalogue record for this book is available from the British Library.

ISBN: 978-0-8264-9847-2 (hardback)
978-0-8264-9848-9 (paperback)

Library of Congress Cataloguing-in-Publication Data
A catalog record for this book is available from the Library of Congress.

Typeset by Servis Filmsetting Ltd, Stockport, Cheshire
Printed and bound in Great Britain by MPG Books Ltd, Bodmin, Cornwall

CONTENTS

NOTE

Emma page references are to the 2003 Penguin Classics paperback.

CHAPTER 1

CONTEXTS

AUSTEN'S LIFE

The fascination with Austen the writer and Austen's work has been consistent since the steady rise of Austen's reputation during the nineteenth century. By 1917, the hundred-year anniversary of her death, Austen was firmly established as an indispensable voice in the canon of British literature. Indeed, it was Austen's novel, *Emma* (1815), that solidified her reputation during her own lifetime, and which served to bring her to an ever-widening audience. In 1816, the most popular writer of the day, the poet and novelist Sir Walter Scott, reviewed *Emma* in the *Quarterly Review*. Although there had been brief and favorable reviews of the earlier novels, *Sense and Sensibility* (1811) and *Pride and Prejudice* (1813), Scott's account of *Emma* triggered a public awareness and celebration of Austen as an innovative and brilliant narrative artist, forging new tools to construct a kind of uncanny realism, new to the novel form. In his review, Scott presents Austen's achievement in *Emma* in terms of her transformation of the novel from a form which explored romance, adventure, and idealized sentiment to one which emphasized "nature as she really exists in the common walks of life." The dramatic power of her characters led some nineteenth-century writers, including Thomas Macaulay and George Lewes, to regard her as no less than a "prose Shakespeare." In the words of George Moore, Jane Austen turned the washtub into the vase; in effect, she transformed the eighteenth-century novel—which could be a clumsy and primitive performance—into a work of art. She invented her own special mode of fiction, the domestic comedy of middle-class manners, a dramatic, realistic account of the quiet backwaters of everyday life for the country families of Regency England from the late 1790s until 1815.

The modesty of Jane Austen's fictional world is caught in her remark to a novel-writing niece that "3 or 4 Families in a Country Village is the very thing to work upon," and her famous comment to a novel-writing nephew about "the little bit (two inches wide) of Ivory on which I work with so fine a Brush" which "produces little effect after much labour." The novels communicate a profound sense of the movement in English history, when the old Georgian world of the eighteenth century was being carried uneasily and reluctantly into the new world of Regency England, the Augustan world into the nineteenth century.

Jane Austen was born near Basingstoke, in the parish of Steventon in the southern English county of Hampshire, on 16 December 1775. She was received into a web of family connections that included on one side the rich and influential Leighs of Stoneleigh Abbey and the Knights of Godmersham and, on the other side, clerics connected to the Church of England and an apprentice milliner. Her father, George Austen, was the rector of Steventon and her mother Cassandra (born Leigh) held aristocratic links through her extended family. George Austen's family connections were also formidable. Through Thomas Knight, the rich husband of George Austen's second cousin, Mr. Austen obtained the parish at Steventon. Thomas Knight owned not only the parish position, or living, to which he helped place George, he also owned the manor at Steventon, with all its dependent houses and holdings. Knight rented to the Austens a nearby farm—part of the Steventon manor—to help further George's clerical income. The farm added about a third to the Austen family's overall income and together, with a reliance on tithes from those lands, the Steventon farm assured that the family would hold a keen interest in agriculture and agricultural improvements. With Thomas Knight a patron to the budding family, the Austens were secure of rank and position in Steventon. To increase his income still further, George took in well-to-do boys to prepare for university with at least four pupils in residence at the rectory by 1779. While common for Anglican clergymen to tutor boys for the additional income, the activity suggests the still insecure financial footing of the Austen family. With the status of her parents delicately balanced on dependence to extended family, land tithes, and on boarder students, one can understand Jane Austen's lifelong concern for money and the nuances of class. As many scholars have noted, the unique position of George Austen's household at once clerical, agricultural, and academic helped to frame the special province of Jane Austen's art.

In Austen's fiction, important as native intelligence and good sense prove, birth and breeding matter still more: the fine gradations of class that inform works like *Emma* are due in part to the complex social world in which Austen grew up. Her father, George, was by all accounts a very learned man, and her mother, Cassandra, too, was famous for her wit and incisive mind. Both, as we have noted, held important family connections, with Mrs. Austen being a notch higher due to her extended family's claims to the aristocracy. The intellectual nature of the household is evident in the extensive library of over 500 volumes possessed by George Austen. Jane Austen's brother Henry observed of their father that he was "a profound scholar" with "most exquisite taste," and Mrs. Austen is frequently noted in the family's surviving papers for her ability in composing witty comic verse on local people and events. Into this intellectually rich and comically inclined home, Jane was born.

George and Cassandra Austen had eight children of which Jane was the seventh. Of the five boys, one child, George, was born handicapped and was sent from home to live in a neighboring community—a common practice at the time for well-to-do parents faced with the challenges of a severely handicapped child. Of the four other boys, the Austen sons were all successful: James followed his father into the Anglican Church and ultimately into the living at Steventon; Edward was adopted by the rich Knight relatives, later changed his name to Knight, and inherited Godmersham Park, Chawton Manor, and Steventon; Francis and Charles entered the Royal Navy Academy as young boys, just under 12 years of age, and rose up the ranks during the Revolutionary and Napoleonic wars, ending as admirals; after a time in the militia Henry became a banker and agent for the army until bankrupted in March 1816 by the post-war economic slump; he then entered the Church. By contrast, the two girls—Jane and her beloved older sister Cassandra—had no professional opportunities and few chances of forming an income. Only through their relationships with their male siblings did the Austen daughters have a chance to take part in the large political, military, and economic tableaux of late eighteenth and early nineteenth-century England. In the same period that the feminist Mary Wollstonecraft was writing her *Vindication of the Rights of Women* (1792) criticizing the restricted lives of women, Jane Austen and her sister Cassandra were living the critique.

If Austen was aware of Wollstonecraft's text, she would have read in it a map for the limits that she faced in her life: the only real "work" that society sanctioned was the gaining of a husband. And, if a young woman, like Jane, remained unmarried (which she did), she was considered a drain on their family, used primarily to help nurture and nurse married relatives. Jane Austen's life would play out according to the limitations Wollstonecraft lamented, but for one significant difference: Jane Austen was an artist of genius and she wrote six novels that have come down to us as some of the finest novels in the English language. Austen accepted the inescapable fact of female dependency on men in her day, and the anger expressed in Wollstonecraft is never directly expressed in her works; rather, that anger was turned to irony and a comic and playful wit that is everywhere on display in Austen and which fuels the success of her novels still.

In 1783, Jane and her sister Cassandra were sent to Oxford to be tutored by Mrs. Ann Cawley, who then took them to Southampton, a stay interrupted by an outbreak of typhus from which Jane nearly died. There followed a couple of years of more formal education at Abbey House School in Reading, ruled by the eccentric Mrs. La Tournelle, known for her cork leg and her obsession for the theater. A writer like Dickens would have found the model for fiction from such an eccentric, and yet it is characteristic of Austen that no character of hers has a cork leg. Austen's mind and art would never be enchanted by outward extremes, but rather hers was an art of interior nuance.

By the end of 1786, after less than three years of formal education, the Austen girls were recalled to Steventon, where they were educated—likely in a better fashion—by their educated father, mother, and brothers. One cannot help but hear Austen voicing her own view of the Reading School years when Emma commends Mrs. Goddard's establishment in Highbury: "a real, honest, old-fashioned Boarding-school, where a reasonable quantity of accomplishments were sold at a reasonable price, and where girls might be sent to be out of the way and scramble themselves into a little education, without any danger of coming back prodigies" (p. 22). Jane Austen's real education would come not from Mrs. La Tournelle and the Reading

School, but from her beloved Hampshire, where among her father's library and amid the family's rich social interactions, she did become a prodigy.

Financially dependent on their father—Jane had only £20 a year to spend on herself or give away to charity—Austen and her sister Cassandra sought marriage as a course to establishing independence. Neither sister achieved it: Cassandra became engaged to Tom Fowle, a clergyman, who died in Jamaica from yellow fever, leaving Cassandra some measure of independence from her father with £1000 a year. Around the time of Cassandra's engagement, Jane briefly flirted with Tom Lefroy, the nephew of her much-loved neighbor Madam Lefroy, who made sure the young man left before his relationship with the penniless Jane became too serious. Famously, the two shared a love and interest in the works of Henry Fielding, especially *Tom Jones*. Of course, it is tempting to imagine the two flirting over the love scenes in Fielding's novel. However little is known about the relationship between Jane and Lefroy, the brief flirtation is the source of much romantic speculation and revisionist history, including the 2007 Miramax film *Becoming Jane*—which imagines far more in the relationship than was likely the case.

Beyond the expected career of husband hunting, which Jane Austen appeared to take seriously, she also embarked on a career as a novelist. Austen began as a child to write novels for her family. Some of her youthful efforts were written as early as 1790. Beginning in about 1795, Jane Austen began to write beyond the gifted juvenilia that had already garnered the attention and appreciation of her family. Around this time, with the encouragement of the gift of a writing desk from her father, Austen began sketching out three full-length novels, the beginning seeds of her three great early works, *Pride and Prejudice*, *Sense and Sensibility*, and *Northanger Abbey*. "First Impressions," the early version of *Pride and Prejudice*, was the first she felt confident enough to consider publishing. With her family's encouragement and guidance, her father offered "First Impressions" to the publisher Thomas Cadell in 1801. Cadell declined to review the manuscript. Before this setback, and with the confidence of having completed "First Impressions," Austen also began on the final version of what would become *Sense and Sensibility*. During this heady period, with the growing knowledge of her own gifts and maturing abilities, Jane Austen faced the news that her parents had decided to move with their two unmarried daughters to Bath. She would be leaving the land and social world that was the core of her emerging literary art.

The Austens moved from Steventon to Bath in 1801. The decision to move was made while Jane Austen was absent from home, and upon learning of the move on her return, Jane is said to have fainted at the news. George Austen appointed his son James as curate of Steventon, sold his farming lease, and decamped for a resort city known for its healing waters and electricity health treatments. It is also likely that the Austen parents considered the move an opportunity to increase the chances of securing husbands for their two unmarried daughters. The family could live comfortably, if not grandly, in lodgings on the tithe income from the Steventon property.

Jane Austen's life in Bath was eventful and very unlike the retired life she led in Steventon. Although she did not have the solitude and quiet she enjoyed at Steventon, she did continue to work. Scholars are uncertain as to whether she began new novels during her time in Bath, but she did continue revising her earlier drafts of what would become *Pride and Prejudice, Sense and Sensibility,* and *Northanger Abby.*

In 1802, while visiting friends back in Hampshire, Jane Austen received a surprise offer of marriage from Harris Bigg-Wither of the Bigg-Wither family, the prosperous, land-owning family of Manydown Park. Throughout Jane and Cassandra's twenties, the young women visited Manydown frequently as part of their intimacy with the three sisters of the Bigg-Wither family and as part of their wider interaction in Hampshire society. Harris Bigg-Wither was only 21 years of age and Jane was almost 27 (the age at which her novels begin to consider her female characters to be spinsters). Austen initially accepted the proposal, only to recant the next morning. The temptation must have been great. By marrying Bigg-Wither, Jane Austen would have become the wife of the heir to a very substantial country house and estate. She would have been able to live comfortably and socially ascendant in the Hampshire neighborhood of her birth, close to all those she loved best. Furthermore, to marry Harris Bigg-Wither would have provided for her sister Cassandra and would have removed the financial burden of two unmarried daughters from the Austen parents in their declining years. Relations between the Austen and the Bigg-Wither families became strained after Austen withdrew her acceptance, but eventually the rift was mended and the Austen and Bigg-Wither sisters renewed their close friendship.

Austen sold her first novel to a publisher in 1803. It was the third of her original draft works, which she titled *Susan* (and which would later become *Northanger Abbey*). The publisher, Crosby and Co., bought the novel outright for a sum of £10. The work was scheduled for publication and advertised, but never brought into print. Toward the end of her life, Austen bought back the manuscript and the work was published posthumously as *Northanger Abbey* in 1818.

George Austen, Jane's father, died in 1805, four years after moving the family to Bath. The loss was devastating to Jane, her sister Cassandra, and their mother. The income remaining to the three after the loss of Mr. Austen totaled only £210 per year, less than a quarter of the income of what would be required if they were to maintain the living arrangements they had enjoyed while Mr. Austen was alive. They spent the next year in Bath shifting to less and less expensive apartments in the effort to stave off absolute poverty, a fate that often befell unmarried and widowed women of Austen's social class. Jane's brothers, Edward, James, and Henry, provided additional income, but the Austen women's income remained less than half of what they had while Mr. Austen lived. The very real threat of poverty convinced the three to leave Bath for good in 1806.

For the next three years, the Austens stayed with various family members and friends and in rented lodgings until 1809, when they moved back to Hampshire into a home of their own at Chawton. Jane's brother Edward owned this home, known as Chawton Cottage, as part of the estates he inherited with the Knight properties in Kent. He provided it as a permanent home for his mother, his sisters, and their friend Martha Lloyd, who lived with the Austen women until her marriage to Frank Austen in 1828. The return to Hampshire and the escape from poverty allowed Jane Austen to focus on her art again. It was while living in Chawton Cottage that Austen completed the revisions of her earlier novels, and where she wrote the remaining works, including her most accomplished novel, *Emma*.

Jane Austen's six complete adult novels were written in two distinct periods. Those of her first period (1796–8) took more than 15 years to revise and to find publishers. During this time she wrote *Sense and Sensibility* (1811), the story of two sisters and their love affairs; *Pride and Prejudice* (1813), the most popular of her novels, dealing with the five Bennet sisters and their search for suitable husbands; and *Northanger Abbey* (1818), a satire on the highly popular Gothic romances of the late eighteenth century.

Austen's second period of productivity began in 1811 after the publication of *Sense and Sensibility*. Following 12 disappointing and unproductive years, including the Bath years, Jane Austen produced in quick succession her last three novels: *Mansfield Park* (1814), *Emma* (1816), and *Persuasion* (1818). All three deal with the romantic entanglements of their strongly characterized heroines.

Emma was the last novel Austen published during her lifetime— and it was the novel that must have given her the greatest sense of her own accomplishment. By that point, her difficulty in getting her work published was behind her. Indeed, Austen chose the fashionable John Murray, publisher of the most celebrated writers of the day, Lord Byron and Walter Scott, to bring out *Emma*. Furthermore, unbidden, the Prince Regent contacted Austen through his librarian and asked that she dedicate her newest work to him. Such an approval was, in fact, essentially an order that such a dedication must be made. Though Austen disapproved of the Prince Regent's personal habits and morals, the solicited dedication assured that *Emma* had received the imprimatur of the royal family, demonstrating the even greater acceptance of her work by the elite of England. Essentially, with the last novel that she would see of her own in print, Austen received a royal seal upon her success as a major author.

During Jane Austen's last year, 1817, while she worked on her last novel, *Persuasion*, she suffered from what would prove a fatal illness. The exact nature of her illness is unknown, though recent medical reviews of the historical record suggest it may have been Hodgkin's disease, or some other lymphoma. Regardless of the specific identity of the disease, the Austen family letters that remain from 1817 indicate the progressive nature of her deterioration. In May 1817, Austen was moved to Winchester, 16 miles from Chawton, so that she could receive better medical attention. She found walking to be difficult and received what little exercise she could by riding on the back of a donkey. She continued to write, however, until shortly before her death. On 18 July 1817, Jane Austen died peacefully in the arms of her sister Cassandra. Asked for her last wishes, she replied, with characteristic dignity, economy, and wit, "I want nothing but death" (*Memoir*, p. 131). Her last written words were a poem on the effect of rain on St. Swithin's day or, in her niece Caroline's phrase, a "joke about the dead Saint and the Winchester races" (in Todd (2006), p. 13). In Austen's poem, St. Swithin mounts the palace roof and declares: "When once we are buried you think we are dead / But behold me immortal" (*Collected Poems*, p. 17). Those final written lines proved prophetic for one of the best-loved novelist in the English language. She was buried in Winchester Cathedral.

THE HISTORICAL CONTEXT

Historically, Austen's novels, including *Emma*, are a challenge to the idea of society as a civilizing force and to the image of man's fulfillment as an enlightened social being. As the Austen scholar Alistair Duckworth has demonstrated, Austen's works question the driving optimism of the period—that English society during the Regency period (1811–20) was triumphantly the Age of Improvement. "Improvement" was the leading spirit of Regency England, its self-awarded palm. Certainly the period was unequaled as a time of economic improvement, in the wake of the industrial revolution. The wartime economy accelerated this new prosperity. Alongside this material improvement there was an air of self-conscious, self-congratulatory improvement in manners, in religious zeal, in morality, in the popularization of science, philosophy, and the arts. It was the age of encyclopedias, displaying the scope and categories of human knowledge in digestible form. Books and essays paraded "Improvement" in their titles.

But, many of the achievements of the Regency period were more apparent than actual. This is nicely symbolized in its most conspicuous manifestation across the countryside itself. Landscape improvement was celebrated as the latest of the fine arts, much theorized about by contemporary aestheticians and brandished as a distinctively English contribution to the sum of civilization. Country houses and their grounds were expensively and elaborately improved, as General Tilney's "improving hand" has transformed the pre-Reformation convent of Austen's *Northanger Abbey* into a modern home of extravagant and faintly ludicrous luxury, and as in Austen's *Mansfield Park*, the fashionable improver of the day, Repton, is to transform Sotherton Court, a fine old Elizabethan country house, destined to be adorned in "a model dress."

Throughout her novels Jane Austen plays deftly with the terminology of improvement, carrying its negative overtones of novelty, showiness, and superficiality into the realms of manners, behavior, and morality. Improvement can be a facade, a veneer. Jane Austen's skeptical, testing irony is the acid solution to peel it off, exposing the ramshackle foundations of social and personal morality which improvement could flashily conceal. Socially and politically, improvement had a very bitter ring for Austen. Essentially it was a middle-class conceit. Consider, for example, Mrs. Elton's continual gushing about the improvement of her sister's and Mr. Suckling's estate, Maple Grove: "Nothing can stand more retired from the road than Maple Grove. Such an immense plantation all round it! You seem shut out from every thing—in the most complete retirement" (p. 286). She compares Maple Grove to Hartfield, home to the Woodhouses: "The laurels at Maple Grove are in the same profusion as here, and stand very much in the same way—just across the lawn; and I had a glimpse of a fine large tree, with a bench round it, which put me so exactly in mind!" (p. 254). And elsewhere:

> [Mrs Elton's] Bath habits made evening-parties perfectly natural to her, and Maple Grove had given her a taste for dinners. She was a little shocked at the want of two drawing rooms, at the poor attempt at rout-cakes, and there being no ice in the Highbury card parties. Mrs Bates, Mrs Perry, Mrs Goddard and others, were a good deal behind hand in knowledge of the world, but *she* would soon shew them how every thing ought to be arranged. In the course of the spring she must return their civilities by one very superior party—in which her card tables should be set out with their separate candles and unbroken packs in the true style—and more waiters engaged for the evening than their own establishment could furnish, to carry round the refreshments at exactly the proper hour, and in the proper order. (p. 269)

Compare this "improving" spirit of Mrs. Elton's and the legacy of Maple Grove to what Emma sees when she looks from Donwell Abbey to the Highbury residence of Mr. Knightley: "The house was larger than Hartfield, and totally unlike it, covering a good deal of ground, rambling and irregular, with many comfortable and one or two handsome rooms.—It was just what it ought to be, and it looked what it was—and Emma felt an increasing respect for it, as the residence of a family of such true gentility, untainted in blood and understanding" (p. 336). Here, Mr. Knightley's home comes to stand for the native and natural "improvement" of the genuine article, "true gentility." The house itself displays moderation, taste, concern for others, and a reluctance to deceive—the very personal qualities that make Mr. Knightley the novel's hero.

Outside the gentry's world of property and privilege was a wholly different scene. Throughout this period a third of the country, its laboring population, lived permanently on the verge of starvation, while the rich became even richer, their prosperity more blatant. In such fertile ground revolutionary ideas took root, and the period from the beginning of the 1790s until the Peterloo Massacre of 1819 was the most violent and repressive time in English history since the Civil War. Habeas corpus was suspended. Freedom of speech and freedom of assembly were curtailed. Bread riots were met with force. Jane Austen gives no more than a fleeting glimpse of such violence. Indeed, in *Northanger Abbey* the London mobs come in as a joke. We never see the grinding misery of the poor in Austen; they are simply objects of charity, to be visited with refreshments and kind words—as Emma and Harriet visit the poor cottagers in *Emma*. It was not that Jane Austen was unaware; Hampshire and Kent, where she spent most of her adult life, were as badly hit by agricultural poverty as any other part of England. She must have seen it for herself and read about it in the essays and pamphlets of crusading reformers; and met it poignantly in her favorite poet, George Crabbe (1754–1832), who delivered a scathing report of what he observed in his widely read poem "The Village" which includes the lines, "the Village of Life a Life of Pain" (Book 2, ln 2).

Ironically, one of Jane Austen's major achievements in the novels is to have captured the total illusion of the gentry's vision, the experience of living in privileged isolation, of being party to a privileged outlook and belonging to a privileged community, whose distresses, such as they are, are private, mild, and genteel. Austen signals as much with the opening lines of *Emma*:

> Emma Woodhouse, handsome, clever, and rich, with a comfortable home and happy disposition, seemed to unite some of the best blessings of existence; and had lived nearly twenty-one years in the world with very little to distress or vex her. (p. 7)

As the novel proceeds we are eased into the genteel community of Highbury, a microcosm, the center of a minute universe—"with very little to distress or vex." The irony is implicit in both Austen's opening sentence and in those that follow. The miniature issues of

Highbury and its genteel class, so realistic, so much the center of the stage, vivid and magnified to the point of surrealism, imply another, larger world beyond. Austen was aware of John Thelwall's *The Peripatetic* (1793) which presented a line of argument that she would weave into her novels: "the flourishing grandeur of a Country, is but another term for the depression and misery of the people . . . to speak of the expensive luxury and refinements of an age, is but, with cruel irony, to remind us how many myriads are destitute" ("National Opulence," 152). "The depression and misery" of the common people was a theme Austen could never handle directly; her way is to treat it by silent implication in such ironic moments as the gypsy attack on Harriet Smith in *Emma* (Chapter 39), Emma's visit to the poor cottage (Chapter 10), and Mrs. Weston's "pilfered poultry" (Chapter 55).

It is with momentary and glancing allusions, then, that Jane Austen reminds the reader of the unseen England beyond the blinkered social focus of the gentry's vision. Austen is more forthcoming about another "depression and misery" that she knew more intimately, and could command fully and creatively. This was the private, personal history of women like herself, trapped and stifled within the confines of a hothouse society, recognizing its brittleness and artificiality, but with no other world to exist in.

For all of its insularity Austen's *Emma* is a book of its time. The novel's publication in December 1815 coincided with a turning point in England's social and political history. The wars with France and fears of foreign invasion were over, and the nation was turning its attention inland, where domestic upheavals were beginning to highlight the fact that England's wealth and, inevitably, its social and political power were redistributing themselves in ways that would shape the nation's consciousness throughout the century and into the next.

Austen captures the uneasy mixture of the middling classes during this time of great change. She populates her novels with them. The upper class appear as established landholders (Mr. Knightley and the Churchills), the professional classes as lawyers (John Knightley), the clergy (Mr. Elton), and the military (Mr. Weston). Here, too, are members of the commercial middle class— traders and bankers (the Fords, the Coles, Mrs. Elton)—growing in wealth and working their way into gentry society though not materially challenging its precepts. Austen even hints at the new industrial middle class, who, as Eric Hobsbawm points out, "did not possess emotional attachments to the old regime" (p. 83) and were more likely to define themselves in stark contrast to the older upper and middle classes—in religion, lifestyle, and values (the Tupmans). Austen maps out this complex social topography and transposes it artlessly onto the little world of Highbury, to "the little bit (two inches wide) of Ivory" on which she works with "so fine a brush." The sure touch by which Austen paints the prejudices, jealousies, and class anxieties of England's shifting social order is nicely summed up in W. H. Auden's verse epistle "Letter to Lord Byron," where Auden confesses a discomfort at finding Austen so sure of hand in presenting her social context:

> You could not shock her more than she shocks me:
> Besides her Joyce seems innocent as grass.
> It makes me most uncomfortable to see
> An English spinster of the middle class
> Describe the amorous effects of "brass",
> Reveal so frankly and with such sobriety
> The economic basis of society.

LITERARY CONTEXT

To talk of Austen's *Emma* in its literary context is to take up Austen's important contributions to the history of the novel. The idea we most commonly associate with novels, the idea of realism, is born in works like *Emma*. Jane Austen did not try to associate her novels with poetry and romance as did other writers such as Sir Walter Scott. Rather, Austen forged a new path: it is to Austen that we are most indebted for the development of the realistic novel.

Sir Walter Scott recognized Austen's break with the past. In his essay on *Emma*, he sets out a truncated history of the novel:

> In its first appearance the novel was the legitimate child of Romance, and though the manner and general tone of style were altered so as to suit modern times, the author remained fettered by many peculiarities of the original style of romantic fiction. The reader expected to pursue a course of adventures more interesting and extraordinary than those that occur in his own life, or that of his next door neighbours. (p. 189)

Scott is beginning to ask questions of the very tradition he had embraced as an artist. What happens, Scott asks, when novels refuse to paint the extraordinary? What happens in reading when we do not escape our small societies, and ourselves, but instead read adventures like those that occur in our own lives? What happens when fiction is not about the extraordinary adventures of a knight-errant, but about the everyday lives of our "next door neighbours?" Before Austen, Scott goes on to say:

> the novelist professed to give an imitation of nature, but it was, as the French say, *La Belle Nature*. Austen's nature may not be *"Belle"* but it is real. Her subjects are not often elegant, and certainly never grand, but they are finished up to nature, and with a precision which delights the reader. (p. 190)

With his own precision, Scott is signaling the revolution in fiction that *Emma* helps instigate, the giant leap forward *Emma* initiates beyond the novelistic traditions of romance, Gothic fiction, and the adventure story. Austen helps shift the kinds of subjects novels can and will represent. In Plato's terms of literary criticism, Scott is speaking here about a change in the objects of *mimesis*, meaning imitational representation. Scott is recognizing Austen's genius in shifting the mimetic field of interest away from the traditions of myth and romance, and to the naturalism of everyday life.

Scott recognized that, with Austen, the novel's subject changes from objects that are noble, or mythological, or fantastic to the familiar and the quotidian. The gift of Austen's genius is that she makes this shift in subject matter appear so effortless. In the small scope of the actions of *Emma*, Austen represents the way people actually experienced living, not only what their lives looked like—the neighborhoods, houses, and landscape of Hartfield—but also the process by which they understand, or fail to understand their lives. Austen's narrative gift captures the justice or injustice of her characters perceptions and the consequences of their actions, including their triumphs and their blunders. Herein lies the appeal of Emma herself, a character designed to be, as Austen said herself, "a heroine whom no one but myself will much like" (*Memoir*, 157). Emma's prejudices, jealousies, and narrowness are naturally depicted, but so too are her generosity of spirit, her humor, and her active sympathy. Austen's heroine may get it wrong, what is worse she may never get it right, yet it is Austen's clear-sighted depiction of human error and conceit that captures the dynamic flux of common life, that makes a character like Emma more real to us than our own neighbors.

Scott recognized Austen's departure from the novelistic tradition that preceded her, and he also intuited the radical break this departure meant for the novel as a vehicle to explore human experience. He describes it thus:

> The second broad line of distinction between the novel as formally composed and real life is the difference of the sentiments. In the serious class of novels, the hero is usually a knight of love who never broke a vow. Although, in those of a more humorous class, he was permitted a license, still a distinction was demanded even from [Tobias Smollett's] Peregrine Pickle and [Henry Fielding's] Tom Jones. The heroine was, of course, still more immaculate. And to have conferred her affection onto any other than the lover to whom the reader had destined her from their first meeting would have been a crime against sentiment, which no author would have hazarded under the old regime. We therefore bestow no mean compliment upon the author of *Emma* when we say the narrative of all her novels is composed of such common occurrences as may have come under the observation of most folks. And her *dramatis personae* conduct themselves upon the motives and principles which the readers may recognize as ruling their own, and that of most of their acquaintances. The kind of moral also which these novels inculcate applies to the path of common life. (p. 200)

Under the old regime, the regime of romance, one doesn't make errors of perception or judgment, especially in those heightened experiences of perception that we call love. The reader recognizes, as the immaculate heroine will, or already does, her hero or true love, and that hero is always worthy of such recognition. Austen's novels and their heroines break with this tradition to forge the tradition of the realistic novel.

STUDY QUESTIONS FOR CHAPTER 1

1. Although *Emma* is not generally considered to be an autobiographical novel, it can be seen as a novel which is indirectly about

Austen's life. In what ways might *Emma* be about Austen's life? How useful is knowledge of Austen's biography in appreciating the novel?

2. Rent and view the popular 2007 film *Becoming Jane*, purportedly based on Jane Austen's life. Consider the presentation of Austen by director Julian Jarrold compared with the factual biography sketched in this chapter. What is newly invented for the silver screen, what is true to the historical facts? Is the film, in spirit, a faithful depiction of Jane Austen the novelist?

3. This chapter has suggested a range of elements from the novel's period, Regency England (1811–20), that provide the historical context for Austen's *Emma*, including the idea that this was The Age of Improvement, shifting power relations between the professional, middling, and landed classes, and the depression and misery of the rural poor. Which of these elements do you think are especially important in Austen's *Emma*, and why are they important? To what extent does knowledge of English society in this period help us understand *Emma*?

4. The romantic novelist Sir Walter Scott was one of the earliest and best Austen critics. What three or four qualities did he find most innovative in Austen's Emma?

CHAPTER 2

LANGUAGE, STYLE, AND FORM

LANGUAGE AND STYLE

As we noted in Chapter 1, the works of Jane Austen are very different in style from the works of romance, Gothic fiction, and adventure produced by her contemporaries. With trenchant observation and in meticulous detail, she presented the quiet, day-to-day country life of the upper-middle-class English. Austen has often been praised for the language and style of her prose. She is also thought to be a master of narrative construction, gifted with an impeccable sense of how to shape and structure a story. Together these narrative arts contribute to her greatest achievement, and her most important contribution to the tradition of the novel: her innovative treatment of human consciousness.

To see what makes Austen's language and style both special and important in *Emma*, we will begin this chapter by exploring at length two representative passages to see how Austen's unique use of language and style unite to create the narrative device of free indirect discourse. Indeed, through her inventive use of free indirect discourse, she paves the way for generations of later writers and provides a compelling image of consciousness itself. We will then turn to a discussion of *Emma*'s form by detailing its features and how these features help develop the comedic tradition of the English novel.

Austen is celebrated as the inventor of free indirect discourse; this is best defined as a mixture between psycho-narration and interior monologue. In traditional third-person narrative, a narrator sets the scene and offers us a character's thoughts from a distance, except when the characters speak in dialogue. In free indirect discourse, the author blends the narrator and characters as "dual voices;" that is, the voices of the narrator and the characters are intertwined. The hallmark of such a device is informal syntax (incomplete sentences, exclamations, dashes, etc.) and the depiction of associative thinking. With free indirect discourse, the focus of the author is not on proper and symmetrical syntax structures, but rather on reproducing the character's interior thoughts and associations, what critics call a character's "mind style." The device can create an impression of immediacy—we enter more fully into the communion of the interior life of the characters—but it can also be used to introduce an element of irony, when the reader realizes that a character is misguided without actually being told so by the narrator.

An example will help clarify. In the opening description of Harriet Smith, we begin by hearing the narrator's voice—Austen's third-person narrator describing Harriet Smith. By the end, however, we are inside Emma's mind, seeing things as she sees them, as if Emma herself is telling us about what is going on around her. The narrator and the consciousness of the character merge:

> Harriet Smith was the natural daughter of somebody. Somebody had placed her, several years back, at Mrs Goddard's school, and somebody had lately raised her from the condition of scholar to that of parlour-boarder. This was all that was generally known of her history. She had no visible friends but what had been acquired at Highbury, and was now just returned from a long visit in the country to some young ladies who had been at school there with her.
>
> She was a very pretty girl, and her beauty happened to be of a sort which Emma particularly admired. She was short, plump, and fair, with a fine bloom, blue eyes, light hair, regular features, and a look of great sweetness; and, before the end of the evening, Emma was as much pleased with her manners as her person, and quite determined to continue the acquaintance.
>
> She was not struck by anything remarkably clever in Miss Smith's conversation, but she found her altogether very engaging—not inconveniently shy, not unwilling to talk—and yet so far from pushing, shewing so proper and becoming a deference, seeming so pleasantly grateful for being admitted to Hartfield, and so artlessly impressed by the appearance of every thing in so superior a style to what she had been used to, that she must have

good sense, and deserve encouragement. Encouragement should be given. Those soft blue eyes, and all those natural graces should not be wasted on the inferior society of Highbury and its connexions. The acquaintances she had already formed were unworthy of her. The friends from whom she had just parted, though very good sort of people, must be doing her harm. (pp. 23–4)

Here we begin in the key of a traditional narrative presentation: Austen's third-person narrator elects to describe Harriet Smith. ("Harriet Smith was the natural daughter of somebody. Somebody had placed her, several years back, at Mrs. Goddard's school, and somebody had lately raised her from the condition of scholar to that of parlour-boarder. This was all that was generally known of her history.") But as the narrative proceeds, the narrative begins to merge with the "mind style" of the work's central consciousness, Emma Woodhouse. ("Emma was as much pleased with her manners as her person, and quite determined to continue the acquaintance.") As the third-person narrator merges with the consciousness and "mind style" of Emma Woodhouse, proper and symmetrical syntax structures break down into asymmetrical modifying clauses. The narrative becomes controlled not by the formal command of the work's third person narrator, but rather by the shifting perceptions of Emma's own thought processes and consciousness. ("[S]he found her altogether very engaging—not inconveniently shy, not unwilling to talk and yet so far from pushing, shewing so proper and becoming a deference, seeming so pleasantly grateful for being admitted to Hartfield, and so artlessly impressed by the appearance of every thing in so superior a style to what she had been used to, that she must have good sense, and deserve encouragement.") The overall effect is to at once bring us more fully into the flow of Emma's thoughts and feelings, and at the same time, allow us—with the assistance of the third-person narrator—to experience the narrator's, not Emma's, intended irony. Harriet Smith, as repeated readings of the novel will make clear, does not have "good sense," for all her good qualities, and should certainly not be "encouraged." Indeed, Emma's "encouragement" of Harriet will lead to Harriet becoming Emma's romantic rival, a key part of the novel's comic plot.

A further example of free indirect discourse will demonstrate just how tricky Austen's style and language can be. Our discussion here follows the initial scholarship of John Sutherland in his article

"Apple-Blossom in June?" (1996, pp. 14–19). Since the publication of *Emma*, critics of the novel have pointed to one supposed blunder in the verisimilitude of Austen's otherwise impeccable depiction of Highbury and its environment: the June apple-blossoms that appear in Chapter 42. The supposed error occurs in the Box Hill picnic scene. The date of the picnic in the text is given precisely. "It was now the middle of June, and the weather fine" (*Emma*, p. 331). The excursion is described as taking place "under a bright mid-day sun, at almost Midsummer" (i.e. around 21 June) (p. 335). Strawberries are in prospect, which confirms the June date. During the course of the picnic, Austen indulges in an extended passage describing a distant view—specifically, Abbey-Mill Farm, which lies some half-a-mile distant, "with meadows in front, and the river making a close and handsome curve around it." The narrative continues, weaving the idyllic view into Emma's tireless matchmaking activities:

> It was a sweet view—sweet to the eye and the mind. English verdure, English culture, English comfort, seen under a sun bright, without being oppressive.
>
> In this walk Emma and Mr Weston found all the others assembled; and towards this view she immediately perceived Mr Knightley and Harriet distinct from the rest, quietly leading the way. Mr Knightley and Harriet!—It was an odd tête-à-tête; but she was glad to see it.—There had been a time when he would have scorned her as a companion, and turned from her with little ceremony. Now they seemed in pleasant conversation. There had been a time also when Emma would have been sorry to see Harriet in a spot so favourable for the Abbey-Mill Farm; but now she feared it not. It might be safely viewed with all its appendages of prosperity and beauty, its rich pastures, spreading flocks, orchard in blossom, and light column of smoke ascending. (p. 338)

James Kinsley offers a note to "in blossom" for the Oxford Classics edition of the novel:

> The anomaly of an orchard blossoming in the strawberry season was noticed by some of the novel's first readers. Jane Austen's niece Caroline wrote to a friend as follows: "There is a tradition in the family respecting the apple-blossom as seen from Donwell Abbey

on the occasion of the strawberry party and it runs thus—That the
first time my uncle . . . saw his sister after the publication of *Emma*
he said, 'Jane, I wish you would tell me where you get those apple-
trees of yours that come into bloom in July.' In truth she did make
a mistake—there is no denying it—and she was speedily apprised
of it by her brother—but I suppose it was not thought of sufficient
consequence to call for correction in a later edition." (p. 444)

One could defend the anachronistic apple-blossom as a liberty taken
with artistic license. But this is not entirely satisfactory with Austen,
the author of *Northanger Abbey*, a novel which castigates Gothic
fiction's offences against observable nature. And, as R. W. Chapman
notes (regarding the anachronistic apple blossom), such mistakes are
"very rare" in Austen's fiction. It was evidently assumed by Jane
Austen's family that no correction was made because the error was
"not thought of sufficient consequence." Such is unlikely; elsewhere
one can find Jane Austen going to some length to authenticate
details in her fiction, for instance, when she put herself to the trouble
to verify details as to whether there was a governor's house in
Gibraltar, for *Mansfield Park*.

If the "apple-blossom in June" error were pointed out to her, why
then did Jane Austen not change it? Sutherland observations are
appropriate here:

"Orchards in leaf" would have been an economical means of
doing so, requiring no major resetting of type. One explanation
is that she did not have time—some eighteen months after the
publication of *Emma* Austen died, in July 1817. A more appealing explanation is that it is not an error at all. It was not changed
because Austen did not believe it was wrong. In order to make
this second case, one should note that there is not one error in the
description ("apple-blossom in June"), but two, and possibly
three. Surely, on a sweltering afternoon in June, there would not
be smoke rising from the chimney of Abbey-Mill Farm? Why
have a fire? And if one were needed for the baking of bread, or
the heating of water in a copper for the weekly wash, the boiler
would surely be lit before dawn, and extinguished by mid-
morning, so as not to make the kitchen in the family's dining-
room unbearably hot. The reference to the "ascending smoke"
would seem to be more appropriate to late autumn. And the

reference to "spreading flocks" would more plausibly refer to the lambing season, in early spring, when flocks enlarge dramatically. It will help at this point to quote the relevant part of the passage again: "It might be safely viewed with all its appendages of prosperity and beauty, its rich pastures, spreading flocks, orchard in blossom, and light column of smoke ascending." What this would seem to mean is that now Harriet is so effectively separated from Mr Robert Martin, the occupant of Abbey-Mill Farm, she is immune to its varying attractions over the course of the year—whether in spring, early summer, midsummer, or autumn. (p. 19)

What Austen offers us, as Sutherland points out, is not a blunder in her vaunted realism, but rather a precise depiction, in the form of a miniature montage, of the turning seasons. Months may come and months may go, but Harriet will not again succumb to a mere farmer. The depiction here, in fact, is not the traditional symmetrical syntax and description of a third-person narrator, but rather a moment of free indirect discourse with its broken continuity and asymmetrical syntax—married to the mind of the novel's chief consciousness, Emma.

Here, as throughout the novel, Austen navigates deftly between representing the inner life of the protagonist, Emma, and the more knowing perspective of the narrator, just as Austen simultaneously relates the stories of Emma the individual and Highbury the society. In the case of the apple-blossom scene, Austen's shifting back and forth between Emma's perspective and the narrator's is at the core of the narrative richness and verisimilitude of her depiction. Emma imagines in the prospect of Abbey-Mill Farm the change of seasons for which she has saved Harriet as Mr. Martin's wife, but what she has in fact imagined for the more astute reader (and narrator) is the very joys and aptness of the surrounding landscape and seasons for just such a one as Harriet. By the novel's end—in an ironic twist shared only by narrator and reader—Harriet will indeed be making her way toward those very apple-blossoms in June.

FORM

In distinguishing *Emma*'s form from the form of other novels, we might note two of its most striking features. The first is *Emma*'s preoccupation with social values and social distinctions. *Emma* describes an entire society, creating a vivid image of the relationships among whole classes of people. It is not surprising, then, that novels like *Emma* are frequently described as the forerunners of modern ethnographies and social histories. Equally important to *Emma*'s form is its interest in human psychology. Whereas plays and films are often forced to concentrate on externals—how a character moves or speaks—novels like *Emma* are free to probe the inner recesses of both mind and heart. By examining the human community of Highbury and the nature of consciousness itself, Austen develops in her readers a deep sympathy and identification with *Emma*'s characters.

Another determining factor on the form of Austen's novel is its comedic ending. Comedic endings are indeed happy endings. But there's more to such endings than meets the eye. In comedic endings, as characters are fit into the larger social order, a sense of harmony and reconciliation is achieved. Because virtue is rewarded and vice is punished, a sense of poetic justice also prevails. Thus, comedic endings offer a vision of the world as well-ordered and generally sympathetic to human needs and desires. Taken together, the dominance of the courtship plot and the comedic ending account for much of what we might call the "Englishness" of the English novel tradition. Austen's *Emma* is a defining precedent for this tradition: the novel ends with three marriages—Emma and Mr. Knightley, Jane Fairfax and Frank Churchill, and Harriet Smith and Robert Martin. Not surprisingly, the last word of the story is "union" (p. 453).

Finally, the form of Austen's *Emma* owes a debt to the plot structures of the two novels upon which *Emma* is based: Fanny Burney's *Camilla* (1796) and Samuel Richardson's *Sir Charles Grandison* (1753). In *Camilla*, the heroine's relationship to the educated and upright Edgar Mandlebert prefigures Emma's relationship to Mr. Knightley. Mandlebert is only 21, but, like Knightley, he sees it as his duty to favor the 17-year-old Camilla with his "counsel." He advises her, for example, against associating with women of doubtful reputation and attending vulgar entertainments, and Camilla professes herself surprisingly grateful for the advice. In *Sir Charles Grandison*, Sir Charles's sister Charlotte points the way to Austen's portrayal of Emma as a heroine who wins love without the exacting moral reformation required in the conduct book tradition.

STUDY QUESTIONS FOR CHAPTER 2

1. Jane Austen is most celebrated for her contribution of free indirect discourse as a narrative strategy. Review the discussion of free indirect discourse in this chapter, and then locate an instance in Austen's novel. Describe the way free indirect discourse functions in your chosen passage. How does the device provide unique insight into the viewpoint of one of the novel's characters?
2. Austen scholars have long debated the possible blunder of having "apple-blossom" appear in June in *Emma*. This chapter has reviewed the case and suggested that the confusion is due to Austen's complex use of free indirect discourse. Are you convinced by the argument? Can you locate any other inconsistencies or blunders in Austen's realistic depiction of Highbury and its environs?
3. Austen's *Emma* is famous for helping to establish the comedic ending as a feature of the English comic novel tradition. Review the discussion in this chapter and provide a list of the qualities one expects in such a comedic ending. Can you name any contemporary television or movie plots that are similarly structured?

CHAPTER 3

READING *EMMA*

Emma is considered the most formally accomplished novel from a novelist famous for her attention to craft. As our examination of the language, style, and form of *Emma* in the previous chapter has suggested, the work is carefully structured. The richness of its structure has given rise to a wide range of interpretations, and we shall survey these critical responses in the next chapter; in this chapter, we shall focus on three primary themes that animate Austen's tale. These themes are:

1. Courtship
2. Conduct
3. Wellbeing

Each theme is played out under the broader rubric of games: word games and social games. We will simultaneously explore Austen's use of word games and social games while we explore the puzzles of courtship, conduct, and wellbeing that help make *Emma* a literary classic.

WORD GAMES AND SOCIAL GAMES

In Chapter 49 of *Emma*, Mr. Knightley makes his declaration of love to Emma Woodhouse. But soft words do not come easy to our "gentleman-hero". He fumbles and hesitates only to recover by saying: "If I loved you less, I might be able to talk about it more" (p. 403). Emma's response mirrors Knightley's offer: she also finds her powers of speech wanting. In the silence that ensues, Mr. Knightley and Emma discover what Austen terms the "complete truth" of "human disclosure:"

"You are silent . . . absolutely silent," Mr Knightley exclaimed, "But you understand me.—Yes, you see, you understand my feelings—and will return them if you can." (pp. 402–3)

Mr. Knightley had begun the interview with the belief that Emma's affections were lost to Frank Churchill, the frivolous and unreliable young man who had played Emma at a game of cross-purposes; Emma had begun with the belief that Mr. Knightley was about to confess his attachment to Harriet Smith, a confession that warms her jealousy and affection. Mistake and misapprehension lead them on. But before Emma can return a response to Mr. Knightley's proposal, she experiences an epiphany that is expressed, like Knightley's proposal, in a mixture of halting speech and confused silence. She realizes "what she had been saying relative to Harriet had all been taken as the language of her own feeling." With the novel at its climax, and the reader and Mr. Knightley awaiting Emma's response, the narrator makes a telling pronouncement:

> Seldom, very seldom, does complete truth belong to any human disclosure; seldom can it happen that something is not a little disguised, or a little mistaken. (p. 404)

Instead of having Emma speak a breathless "yes," or "I have always loved you too, George," Austen has the narrator discourse on what comprises "complete truth." The moment provides the key to the scene, and to Austen's art. Little disguises and mistakes are essential to the expression of truth—in this case to the expression of our hero and heroine's love.

> [Mr Knightley] had come, in his anxiety to see how she bore Frank Churchill's engagement, with no selfish view, no view at all, but of endeavouring, if she allowed him an opening, to soothe or to counsel her.—The rest had been the work of the moment, the immediate effect of what he heard, on his feelings. (p. 404)

"Complete truth [in] human disclosure" springs unbidden here, but only through the disguises that make disclosure possible. Indeed, little mistakes and disguises permeate the famous love-making scene, extending to the lovers a fresh understanding of their feelings and surprising them with the strength of their own affections.

Mr. Knightly believes Emma is at a loss for words because of her affection for Frank, while Emma sees in Mr. Knightley's fumbling speech a sign of his love for Harriet. These mistakes work to surprise the friends into recognizing and proclaiming their love for one another. For both Emma and Mr. Knightley, silence and halting speech signify a re-interpretation of their conduct and the conduct of others:

> *Her* change was equal.—This one half hour had given to each the same precious certainty of being beloved, had cleared from each the same degree of ignorance, jealousy, or distrust. (p. 405)

By misdirection, direction is found out. Before the end of the chapter, Emma will accept Mr. Knightley. The novel will end comically with the word "union"—as the novel's sets of couples make their way to the altar, each marrying according to their station in life.

But what did Emma say to Mr. Knightley's proposal? Good question:

> "What did she say?" [Austen writes], "Just what she ought, of course. A lady always does." (p. 404)

In Austen's *Emma* "human disclosure" can provide "complete truth" only through disguise and delay. Indeed, disguise and delay are the very tools Austen uses to surprise her readers into re-appraising, like Emma and Mr. Knightley, "love, ignorance, jealousy, and distrust." ("This one half hour had given to each the same precious certainty of being beloved, had cleared from each the same degree of ignorance, jealousy, or distrust.") By playing a complex game of word puzzles and social snakes and ladders, Austen invites the reader to interpret the "complete truth" of the multifaceted themes her work explores: courtship, conduct, and wellbeing.

COURTSHIP

Courtship is the central theme of *Emma*. Indeed, the plot is wholly structured around interlocking sets of courtships: Robert Martin courts Harriet Smith, Mr. Elton courts Emma, Emma courts Mr. Elton on behalf of Harriet, Frank Churchill courts Jane Fairfax and (apparently) Emma, Mr. Elton and Mrs. Elton court each other,

Emma courts (albeit it only lightly) Frank Churchill, Jane Fairfax courts Frank Churchill, Harriet Smith courts nearly everyone: Robert Martin, Mr. Elton, Frank Churchill, and Mr. Knightley. Finally, Mr. Knightley courts Emma and Emma courts Mr. Knightley. These interlocking courtships function as interconnecting rings that, accordion-like, expand and compress as the story draws to a close. Much of the pleasure of reading *Emma* comes from the astonishing way in which Austen works these materials in a narrative shell game of anticipation and surprise.

The first game of courtship played out in the text sets the stage for those that follow, while also providing the theme of courtship to the work as a whole: Mr. Elton courts Emma, while Emma courts Mr. Elton on behalf of Harriet. A short review of this courtship plot is useful here. In the novel, Harriet is the natural daughter of some mysterious person, and Emma, believing that she might be of noble family, persuades Harriet that the society in which she has moved is not good enough for her. Emma encourages Harriet to give up her acquaintance with the Martin family, respectable farmers of some substance though of no fashion. Instead of thinking of Robert Martin as a husband for Harriet, Emma influences Harriet to aspire to Mr. Elton, the young rector. She is certain that Mr. Elton is as much in love with Harriet as Harriet—through Emma's instigation – is with him. Emma suffers a rude awakening when Mr. Elton takes advantage of finding himself alone with Emma in a carriage and asks her to marry him. Emma suddenly realizes that what she had taken for gallantries to Harriet had been meant for her, and what she had intended as encouragement to his suit of her friend, he has taken as encouragement to aspire to Emma's hand. The first set of interlocking courtship games has begun!

The sociologist Johan Huizinga notes: "Real civilization cannot exist in the absence of a certain play-element, for civilization presupposes limitations and mastery of the self, the ability not to confuse its own tendencies with the ultimate and highest goal, but to understand that it is enclosed within certain bounds freely accepted" (1950, p. 211). Jane Austen's *Emma* employs not only the game motif but also game structures. More importantly, the play of mind, the playfulness that is the defining characteristic of *Emma*'s style, testifies to Austen's belief in the essentially creative nature of play. Huizinga's distinctions between "true play" ("its aim is in itself, and its familiar spirit is happy inspiration," (ibid.)) and "false play" ("used consciously or unconsciously to cover up some social . . . design," (p. 205)) apply to *Emma* and its characters. Austen always plays true; her characters generally play false.

For this reason, Austen's novel *Emma* turns time and time again to the genre of riddle and charade to express in miniature the art of human disclosure practiced in its plot. As with a charade or any word puzzle, the significance and power rest not so much in a specific "answer," but rather in the surprise built into the discovery process. As we know, we never get Emma's specific "answer" to Mr. Knightley. We only know it is "just what it ought to be,", that is, what we would have it. The same holds true for the first courtship game of the novel. The game will end with its two chief participants, Emma and Mr. Elton, stunned by a sudden revelation. Like the revelation that closes the Emma and Knightley's courtship plot at the end of the book, the result of the first courtship plot is speechlessness:

> Wthout knowing when the carriage turned into Vicarage-lane, or when it stopped, [Emma and Mr Elton] found themselves, all at once, at the door of his house; and he was out before another syllable passed . . . (p. 126)

The emphasis is on the process of discovery rather than on a speakable answer.

Here some distinctions of genre are useful. The case and the riddle are literary categories that were isolated for study by Andre Jolles in *Einfache Formen* (1972, pp. 137–58). The case evolves as a literary form from law, courtly love, and theology; it emphasizes the mind's ability to propose solutions to difficult problems and solve them so as to allow life to continue within an orderly society. The appearance of the case in a novel gives substance to Hayden White's contention that "narrative in general, from the folktale to the novel . . . has to do with topics of law, legality, legitimacy, or, more generally, *authority*" (1980, p. 17). Whereas the case admits of more than one approach and resolution, the riddle does not. The riddle evolves from magic and religion, is seemingly insolvable, and punishes failure to produce the one right answer to it. The form of the riddle is like that of an examination in which only one answer is acceptable. The examiner asks a question that the one examined must answer or else fail the examination. The riddle therefore produces constraint. In the Sphinx's riddle (Question: What is that which walks on four legs, and two legs, and three legs? Answer: Man: a baby crawls, an adult walks upright, and an elderly person uses a cane) the constraint is clear: Oedipus must solve it or die. When he does solve it, the Sphinx dies. The riddle is the "unwelcome cipher" that Edward Said finds "at the beginning of the quest, the end of which is 'decipherment'" (1975, p. 221).

In the courtship games of *Emma*, Austen succeeds in demonstrating the inextricable link between case and riddle. Austen's "courtship" charade early in the novel proves a miniature lesson for the larger moral "case" demonstrated by the work's various games of courtship. To understand this further, let us focus on the specifics involved in the courtship game played out between Emma, Mr. Elton, and Harriet. This initiating case and riddle sets the precedent for all the other interlocking courtship games played in the novel.

The case is expressed as plot. Emma cannot help but discover Mr. Elton's true intentions when he presses his suit on the return carriage ride from the party at Randalls (Chapter 15):

> [S]carcely had they passed the sweep-gate and joined the other carriage, than she found her subject cut up—her hand seized—her attention demanded, and Mr Elton actually making violent love to her: availing himself of the precious opportunity, declaring sentiments which must be already well known, hoping—fearing—adoring—ready to die if she refused him . . . Mr Elton, the lover of Harriet, was professing himself *her* love. (p. 123)

Emma's astonishment gives way to rebuke. She responds:

> "Command yourself enough to say no more, and I will endeavour to forget it."

But Mr. Elton cannot be refused so easily; as he is sure of the encouragement he has received, even in light of Emma's claim that the encouragement was Mr. Elton's toward her friend Harriet. Mr. Elton says:

> "Charming Miss Woodhouse! Allow me to interpret this interesting silence. It confesses that you have long understood me." (p. 124)

The case, here, might be transcribed thus: "in courtship one may become blinded by self-interest and wish fulfillment and mistake the identity of things." Such a case is the literal unfolding of Austen's plot. The true state of the affair between the pair is only made apparent when both Emma and Mr. Elton accept this truth. No more "interesting silence[s]" by either Emma or Mr. Elton can be interpreted and ventriloquized to project designs and projects once they accept the truth and wisdom of the case. By admitting the case, the facts become apparent: Mr. Elton hopes to catch Emma as a bride that will elevate him socially and financially, while Emma hopes to catch Mr. Elton for Harriet Smith to elevate her. Both find themselves insulted and silenced by the other's presumption.

The game of courtship among Emma, Harriet, and Mr. Elton, then, produces the novel's first case: a case of mistaken identity. In the tradition of law, courtly love, and theology, this case of mistaken identity stands as a kind of parable, or precedent for the blinding power of self-interest and wish fulfillment at the heart of the novel's other games of courtship.

> It was a wretched business, indeed!—Such an overthrow of everything [Emma] had been wishing for! . . .
>
> How she could have been so deceived!—He protested that he had never thought seriously of Harriet—never! She looked back as well as she could; but all was confusion. She had taken up the idea, she supposed, and made everything bend to it . . .
>
> . . . [T]he charade!—and an hundred other circumstances;—how clearly they had seemed to point at Harriet To be sure, the charade . . . (p. 127)

The case of mistaken identity is disclosed and all that is left for Emma to do is to "look back as well as she could," to a "hundred other circumstances" including "the charade!" The "charade" in question is, in fact, the riddle that discloses, in advance, the case of mistaken identity for which Emma is an unwittingly a victim.

If Emma demonstrates the case—"in courtship one may become blinded by self-interest and wish fulfillment and mistake the identity of things"—she also directs the reader's attention back to the riddle that proves a miniature lesson for the larger moral "case" that she has just demonstrated. The "charade" is the riddle that Mr. Elton offers for inclusion in Harriet Smith's book of charades in Chapter 9.

To Miss ————.
CHARADE.

My first displays the wealth and pomp of kings,
Lords of the earth! their luxury and ease.
Another view of man, my second brings,
Behold him there, the monarch of the seas!

But, ah! united, what reverse we have!
Man's boasted power and freedom, all are flown;
Lord of the earth and sea, he bends a slave,
And woman, lovely woman, reigns alone.

Thy ready wit the word will soon supply,
May its approval beam in that soft eye!

As Joseph Litvak has observed, the misreading of this puzzle begins even before Emma reads the charade, as soon as she tells Harriet: "Take it, it is for you. Take your own" (*Emma*, p. 71, Litvak 1985, p. 159). At this point, neither knows what the puzzle says. They only know that it comes from the hand of Mr. Elton. Still, Emma insists on placing the ownership of the puzzle into Harriet's possession ("[t]ake your own"). Emma's phrase "[t]ake your own" betokens her desire to officiate over the courtship that she is arranging. Like a minister joining hands in a wedding ceremony, Emma places the riddle into Harriet's custody.

The scene that follows is one of interpretation and conjecture as Emma and Harriet puzzle out the meaning of Mr. Elton's charade:

> [Emma] cast her eye over it, pondered, caught the meaning, read it through again to be quite certain, and quite mistress of the lines, and then passing it to Harriet, sat happily smiling, and saying to herself, while Harriet was puzzling over the paper in all the confusion of hope and dullness, "Very well, Mr Elton, very well, indeed. I have read worse charades. *Courtship*—a very good hint. I give you credit for it. This is feeling your way. This is saying very plainly— 'Pray, Miss Smith, give me leave to pay my addresses to you. Approve my charade and my intentions in the same glance.' " (p. 70)

Harriet, in her "confusion of hope and dullness," has difficulty deciphering the puzzle, leaving the interpretation to Emma, who obliges:

"For Miss ————, read Miss Smiith.

My first displays the wealth of pomp and kings,
   Lords of the earth! their luxury and ease.

That is *court*.

Another view of man, my second brings,
   Behold him there, the monarch of the seas!

That is *ship*;—plain as can be.—Now for the cream.

But ah! united (*courtship*, you know,) what reverse we have!
   Man's boasted power and freedom, all are flown.
Lord of the earth and sea, he bends a slave,
   And woman, lovely woman, reigns alone.

A very proper compliment!—and then follows the application, which I think, my dear Harriet, you cannot find much difficulty in comprehending . . . There can be no doubt of its being written for you and to you."

The ironies, paradoxes, and importance of this charade and its value to Austen's design cannot be overstated. As the puzzle to the case of mistaken identity, Mr. Elton's charade extends far beyond the literal lesson of the case. Indeed, "in courtship one may become blinded by self-interest and wish fulfillment and mistake the identity of things"—Emma literally realizes this truth without knowing it. ("[T]hen follows the application, which I think, my dear Harriet, you cannot find much difficulty in comprehending . . . There can be no doubt of its being written for you and to you.") Harriet has much "difficulty in comprehending" the charade's apparent "*courtship*" of herself, and, of course, once she is made to comprehend it as Emma does, Harriet has "difficulty" in freeing herself from its hold. Harriet will mourn the loss of Mr. Elton for many chapters. But what Emma fails to see is the obvious ways in which Mr. Elton's charade betrays the deeper game of his quest for Emma's hand. Mr. Elton's riddle reveals his profound concern with "wealth and pomp," "power and freedom." Announcing his interest in "*courtship*," Elton at the same time discloses a preoccupation with "power" (court) and "Wealth" (naval commerce/ship), as well as a design on Emma's money ("luxury and ease"). The deep design of Mr. Elton's riddle forms a kind of logical equation:

"Power" + "Wealth" + "luxury and ease" = "*courtship*"

In setting his sights on Emma, Mr. Elton has clearly done his math.

Ironically, Harriet's apparent blunders in responding to the puzzle come much closer to reading Mr. Elton's riddle properly—and indeed, Harriet succeeds, as no other character does, in disclosing the secret impulses behind the other games of courtship that will be played in the novel after this one closes. Harriet responds to the charade thus:

> "What can it be, Miss Woodhouse?—what can it be? . . . I never saw any thing so hard. Is it kingdom? . . . Can it be woman?
>
> And woman, lovely woman, reigns alone.
>
> Can it be Neptune?
>
> Behold him there, the monarch of the seas!
>
> Or a trident? Or a mermaid? Or a shark? Oh, no! shark is only one syllable . . . Oh! Miss Woodhouse, do you think we shall ever find it out?"

Emma responds:

> "Mermaids and sharks! Nonsense! My dear Harriet, what are you thinking of? Where would be the use of his bringing us a charade made by a friend upon a mermaid or a shark?" (p. 71)

Where Emma reads in Mr. Elton's charade a genial opening to the courtship of a social inferior (Mr. Elton courting Harriet), Harriet finds difficulty ("I never saw any thing so hard"). Instead, Harriet discovers in the puzzle "kingdom," "woman," "Neptune," "A trident," "a mermaid," and finally "a shark." After uncovering these artifacts in Mr. Elton's riddle, she seeks Emma's assistance in discerning how these elements cohere. ("[D]o you think we shall ever find it out?")

Harriet's translation of the riddle as a design related to "kingdom," "woman," "Neptune," "A trident," "a mermaid," and a "shark," ironically captures the deeper game behind Mr. Elton's puzzle ("Power" + "Wealth" + "luxury and ease" = "*courtship*"). Indeed, Harriet's response demonstrates a guarded reaction that would have served Emma well. The astute reader (or re-reader) can assemble from Harriet's first guess, "kingdom," an astute understanding of the "power" and "Wealth" that animate Mr. Elton's desire:

"kingdom" + "power" + "Wealth" = desire

In response to a charade seeking two syllables, Harriet's second answer of "woman" invites the cautionary tale of associating "woe" with "man":

"woe" + "man" = "wo[e]man"

Her third try, "Neptune" and her fourth, "A trident" sketch the myth of the Roman fertility god, Neptune, who is also the god of the Sea and Earthquakes, which he causes by splitting boulders with his trident. Known for his contrariness, temper, and vengeful nature, "Neptune" is not prepossessing in the context of *"courtship:"*

"Neptre" + "A trident" = contrariness, temper, and a vengeful nature

"A mermaid," Harriet's fifth response, signals the legendary aquatic creature with the head and torso of a human female and the tail of a fish. Significantly, mermaids were noted in British folklore as both ominous, foretelling disaster, and provoking it. Several variants of the British folk ballad *Sir Patrick Spens* depict a mermaid speaking to the doomed ships. Again, in the context of *"courtship,"* Harriet's reading betokens trouble:

"A mermaid" = foretelling disaster and provoking it

The "maid" that is separated out as a second syllable response to "mermaid" is particularly ominous for Harriet as a woman who thinks she is being courted by her social superior.

"A mermaid" = "a maid"

Finally, "shark"—though only one syllable ("Oh no!" Harriet responds)—proves a fitting close to her set of ominous interpretations.

Harriet Smith—far more than Emma Woodhouse—sees into Mr. Elton's puzzle. Where for Harriet Mr. Elton's puzzle of *"courtship"* is teaming with ominous signs—"woe," "man," "Neptune," "trident," "mermaid," "maid," and "a shark"—Emma can only see in the puzzle "very proper compliment!" "Mermaid and sharks!" she concludes, "Nonsense!" And yet Harriet's "[n]onsense" lays bare the marriage market that is civilly denoted as *"courtship"* in Mr. Elton's puzzle. Mr. Elton is not rich and he is angling to find a bride who can bring him money in marriage. Again, he has done the math, and, indeed, he captures what he seeks before the novel is halfway complete when he makes Miss Hawkins (and her £10,000 pounds) Mrs. Elton. The "shark" gets his prey.

Although Mr. Elton is by no means set up as a hero in *Emma*—in fact, it would be easy to argue that he and Mrs. Elton are the only villains in the novel—there is a real way in which Mr. Elton points the way to the other characters in the book. As one of Austen's chief riddlers (along with Frank Churchill, as we will see), Mr. Elton's actions initiate the series of courtship games that lead the novel's eligible couples, one by one, to the altar. Mr. Elton marries first, and without scruple, and he does so to assist himself materially. An argument could be made that the other eligible characters in the novel will essentially follow Mr. Elton's lead. They, too, will accept the math behind *"courtship."*

"Power" + "Wealth" + "luxury and ease" = *"courtship"*

Jane Fairfax accepts Frank Churchill, even though he has flirted with Emma and shown himself to be a "shark." She does so because her only other alternative is to become a poor governess. Frank Churchill follows through on his secret engagement to Jane Fairfax because, fortuitously, his aunt, Mrs. Churchill, has died and she can no longer stand in his way. With her death, Frank's fortune is assured, though he cannot enjoy it under the moral cloud of jilting a pledged lover. Emma Woodhouse accepts the middle-aged Mr. Knightley when it becomes clear that the number of eligible young men in Highbury has dwindled. By marrying Mr. Knightley, Emma becomes the first lady of Highbury. Should the marriage prosper, her first-born child will secure the combined properties of Donwell Abbey and Hartfield. (Incidentally, the eldest child of John Knightley and Isabella, Emma's sister, will be cut out.) Mr.

Knightley marries Emma, the 21-year-old woman he has had his eye on since she turned 13, despite the fact that she ignores most of his moral instruction. In doing so, Mr. Knightley will consolidate Donwell Abbey and its farming properties with the contiguous property of Hartfield. His favorite pastime of going over his accounts with his overseer William Larkins will be further enlivened by its improved balance sheet.

Push beyond the civility of the novel's charade, and Harriet Smith is right to perceive "*courtship*" as a calculating affair full of "hard" math. Only Harriet, who marries her first love, Robert Martin, finds out what it all means ("[D]o you think we shall ever find it out?") If "in courtship one may become blinded by self-interest and wish fulfillment and mistake the identity of things," one may also take the blinders off and swim with the sharks.

As Austen's narrator puts it, just as Mr. Knightley ("Neptune") awaits a response of his offer of marriage from Emma ("A mermaid"):

Seldom, very seldom, does complete truth belong to any human disclosure; seldom can it happen that something is not a little disguised, or a little mistaken.

The untangling of the first case of mistaken identity in *Emma*, far from solving, or answering the riddle of "*courtship*" only serves to expand the puzzle outward to encompass the other games of courtship in the novel. Emma says as much: "Receive it on my judgment. It is a sort of prologue to the play, a motto to the chapter, and will be soon followed by matter-of-face prose" (p. 72). Everybody gets caught in its net.

CONDUCT

Another major theme that Austen plays out among Emma's various puzzles and games is the theme of conduct. Behavior that we term "conduct" denotes a broad range of activity under the guidance of social–moral norms. In *Emma*, right conduct is of the utmost importance, precisely because right conduct demonstrates and affirms the social–moral norms upon which society is based. Wrong conduct (or "blunders," as Austen frequently designates the term) is a threat to the guiding codes of race, class, and gender that help imagine and instate social and political boundaries. As we have already seen, the various courtship games of Austen's text challenge and deconstruct some of the polite codes that make up right conduct in Regency England. By explicitly emphasizing conduct as a theme in *Emma*, Austen extends the challenges of her courtship puzzles by further exposing the logic behind other social and political codes. Just as Austen's game of courtship riddles exposes the material calculus of Regency marriage ("Power" + "Wealth" + "luxury and ease" = "*courtship*"), so, too, Austen's game of "blunders" (or wrong conduct) serves to subvert the gender equation that places women subordinate to men in reason.

To trace the development of conduct as a theme in *Emma*, we must first survey Austen's relationship to the genre of conduct literature. Austen developed *Emma* with the popular tradition of conduct literature in mind. The idea that a novel should serve as a guide to social behavior was inescapable for a female novelist in Regency England. Indeed, the conduct novel was the most popular mode of fiction for a female writer at the time. Austen read with interest the popular works of Hannah More and Maria Edgeworth —conduct novelists whose works greatly outsold Austen's in the nineteenth century (see Chapter 4). It was from Hannah More and Maria Edgeworth that Austen learned the shortcoming of conduct fiction, and it was in her attempt to address these shortcomings that she arrived at the theme of conduct and the character of Mr. Knightley for *Emma*.

Unlike Hannah More and Maria Edgeworth, however, Austen refused to subordinate the pleasure of a realistic narrative to direct moral instruction. More's conduct novel *Coelebs in Search of a Wife* (1809) struck Austen as ridiculous (*Letters*, pp. 169–70). Edgeworth's more psychologically nuanced work Austen could admire: "I have made up my mind to like no Novels really, but Miss Edgeworth's, Yours & my own," Austen wrote to her niece Anna (*Letters*, p. 112). Edgeworth had pioneered novels in the tradition of the conduct book, like More, but she had managed a richer art of characterization, though still the unity of interest was achieved by subordinating the events of the novel to the teaching of a moral lesson.

Before *Emma*, Austen seems to have identified herself as writing novels in the tradition of Edgeworth, judging from the titles of her first two published works: *Sense and Sensibility* and *Pride and Prejudice*. Indeed, *Courtship and Conduct* would have made a fitting title for *Emma*. But Austen's artistic gifts and aesthetic sensibilities worked against following Edgeworth towards writing traditional conduct novels like More. Indeed, the tendency in all of Austen's writings, including her juvenilia and letters, is to reverse the process: Austen subordinates the teaching of a moral lesson to the unity of interest found in realistic characterization. Her recognition that her artistic gifts were taking her in a new direction can be found in the titles of the three novels she arranged for publication before her death: *Mansfield Park*, *Emma*, and *Northanger Abbey*.

Austen's innovative brand of the realistic novel, as opposed to the conduct novel popular in her day, can be glimpsed in her literary encounter with Thomas Gisborne's popular conduct book *Enquiry into the Duties of the Female Sex* (1797), and the subsequent use she made of this encounter in *Emma*. Austen was unexpectedly "pleased" by Gisborne's conduct book (*Letters*, p. 112), but where there is a coincidence of opinion between her and Gisborne, Austen's use of such a shared opinion in her novel proves very different from the conduct novel tradition. For instance, Austen would have assented to the distinction that Gisborne makes between a healthy spirit of "emulation," and the destructive effects of "rivalship": "We are all prone to harbour unkind sentiments toward those by whom we feel ourselves surpassed, especially if we were for some time level with them in the race. We find it more easy to depreciate than to equal them" (*Enquiry*, p. 70). Although Austen clearly gives us an example of Emma "harbour[ing] unkind sentiments" toward Jane Fairfax, to whom she does feel herself "surpassed," the same holds true for her conduct hero, Mr. Knightley, who also "harbour[s] unkind sentiments" toward Frank Churchill by whom he too feels himself "surpassed." And like Emma, Mr. Knightley will also find it "more easy to depreciate than to equal." The truth of Gisborne's statement can only be realized when it is played out in the fraught complexities of the relationship between Emma and Jane Fairfax and Mr. Knightley and Frank Churchill. "Emulation" and "rivalship" cannot be easily separated in these relationships—as it cannot be in real life. The truth of Gisborne's wisdom has no power until it is placed in a human context. In Austen's novel, Emma and Mr. Knightley work not simply to become examples of Gisborne's truism regarding "emulation" and "rivalship," rather they demonstrate the value that can be gleaned by activating Gisborne's precepts within the tableaux of realistic fiction.

Again, Austen turns to games and riddles to play out a theme. Like Mr. Elton's "*courtship*" riddle, Frank's "*blunder*" puzzle serves a major role. To understand the subtlety of the puzzle, a short review of the Frank Churchill–Jane Fairfax plot is necessary. Frank Churchill, Mr. Weston's son by his first marriage, has promised for months to come see his father and new stepmother, Emma's former governess. But it is not until Jane Fairfax arrives in Highbury that Frank finally makes his long waited appearance. Jane Fairfax, niece of the garrulous Miss Bates, is Emma's rival in beauty and accomplishment, one reason why, as Mr. Knightly hints, Emma has never been friendly with Jane. Emma herself blames Jane's reserve for their somewhat cool relationship. When Frank Churchill appears, Emma finds him a handsome, well-bred young man. He calls frequently upon the Woodhouses, and also upon the Bates family, because of a prior acquaintance with Jane Fairfax. Emma, rather than Jane, is the recipient of his gallantries, however, and Emma can see that Mr. and Mrs. Weston are hoping that a romance will materialize. About this time Jane Fairfax receives the handsome gift of a pianoforte, anonymously given. It is presumed to have come from some rich friends with whom Jane, an orphan, has lived, but Jane herself seems embarrassed with the present and refuses to discuss it. Emma conjectures, in consultation with Frank Churchill, that the gift signals Jane's inappropriate attachment to Mr. Dixon, husband of Jane's best friend and adopted sister. The gift is actually from Frank. The impropriety of Frank's gift as well as his continued flirtation with Emma begins to place a strain on his relationship to Jane, while making Mr. Knightley apprehensive that Emma reciprocates Frank's interest.

The Frank Churchill–Jane Fairfax plot is poignantly replicated in the game of anagrams that Frank Churchill conducts. All the chief characters are present. Like a modern day game of Scrabble, the reader, like the contestants, is encouraged to unscramble and find value in series of mixed letters and words:

> Frank Churchill placed a word before Miss Fairfax. She gave a slight glance around the table, and applied herself to it. Frank was next to Emma, Jane opposite them—and Mr Knightley so placed as to see them all; and it was his object to see as much as he could, with as little apparent observation. The word was discovered, and with a faint smile pushed away . . . The word was *blunder*; and

Harriet exultingly proclaimed it, there was a blush on Jane's cheek which gave it a meaning not otherwise ostensible. Mr Knightley connected it with the dream; but how it could all be, was beyond his comprehension. (p. 326)

As Joseph Litvak notes in his extensive reading of the scene, the chief competitors are Mr. Knightley and Frank Churchill. Mr. Knightley dislikes Frank Churchill, not only because the younger man seems to be a rival for Emma's affections, but also because Frank presumes to "read every body's character" (1985, p. 141). Having just let slip a possible clue to his involvement with Jane Fairfax, and regretting his carelessness, Frank uses the word game as a pretext for apology. Litvak's interpretation of the scene is worth quoting at length:

As Knightley's stance here shows, his resentment of Frank stems in part from his fear that Frank may usurp the role of master reader: it is Knightley alone who shall reserve the right 'to read every body's character,' to be 'so placed as to see them all.' Knightley's motives here are typical; if Emma, as many critics have noted, is a detective novel, then Knightley, even more than Emma herself, aspires to the role of chief detective. For while Emma is content to fantasize about various romantic scenarios involving Frank Churchill, Knightley will not rest until he has seen into the heart of the mystery surrounding Frank and Jane. For Knightley, reading fosters 'strength of mind,' but is also a mode of surveillance. (ibid., p. 765)

Here, as with Mr. Elton's "*courtship*" riddle, Austen draws her chief characters around the interpretation of a puzzle at the center of which is a key term: this time "*blunder*." Here, too, as in the "*courtship*" riddle it is the unassuming Harriet who discovers the meaning and announces it to Austen's reader and to the others assembled, including Mr. Knightley. ("The word was *blunder*; and Harriet exultingly proclaimed it.") The irony is that Mr. Knightley—Austen's conduct hero—try as he might, cannot decipher the meaning and value of "*blunder*." Even after "plac[ing himself] as to see them all; and it was his object to see as much as he could, with as little apparent observation," he still fails to understand Frank Churchill's game: "[H]ow it could all be, was beyond his comprehension." Read as Austen's ironic treatment of the traditional conduct novel, the scene become more and more comic. Like More's and Edgeworth's heroes, Mr. Knightley does not literally know what a *"blunder"* means (though unlike More's and Edgeworth's heroes, Mr. Knightley is unwittingly guilty of many blunders in the course of the novel). As a traditional conduct hero, he is constitutionally alien to the value and pleasure to be found in a blunder. The puzzling *"blunder"* which escapes Mr. Knightley's understanding is parallel to the earlier *"courtship"* riddle that escapes Emma's notice. If the *"courtship"* riddle conceals a lesson for Emma ("Power" + "Wealth" + "luxury and ease" = *"courtship"*), the *"blunder"* puzzle conceals a lesson for Mr. Knightley (right conduct is predicated on a blunder). Like Emma before him, however, Mr. Knightley will have to suffer the lesson before he can realize it.

Mr. Knightley's anger toward Frank Churchill throughout the novel ("[h]is letters disgust me") signal something more than simple jealousy. Indeed, even before he apprehends Frank Churchill as a rival, Mr. Knightley develops a deep dislike. Mr. Knightley's vehemence strikes Emma as "unworthy the real liberality of mind which she was always used to acknowledge in him" (p. 142). The antipathy is partly generic on Austen's part. Frank Churchill is the anti-Knightley; that is, he is the opposite of the conduct hero. In the tradition of conduct literature and conduct novels like More's and Edgeworth's, Frank is a villain associated with the rake from earlier literature. The rake character is primarily defined by his sexual nature. A rake was concerned about his status among other men. He spent most of his time in search of sexual liaisons or relating tales of past sexual escapades. Harold Weber, a leading scholar on the rake figure, explains: "most rakes possess little identity outside of the love game, their lives responding largely to the rhythms of courtship and seduction, pursuit and conquest, foreplay and release." However, as Weber further points out "the rake is too complex and enigmatic a figure to be reduced to a sexual machine: his love of disguise, need for freedom, and fondness for play all establish the complexity of the rakish personality" (1986, p. 3). The rake's sexual desires can be seen as a call for freedom and a break from social order. He balks at the idea of marriage and family in pursuit of personal gratification. In the works of Austen's peers, More and Edgeworth, the business of the heroine is to remain clear of the threat posed by the rake. She is aided in her struggle through the diligent protection of the conduct hero.

Austen's Frank Churchill is a send-up of this tradition. If Mr. Knightley is, in part, a parody of the conduct hero, Frank Churchill is a reworking of the rake. In this light, we begin to perceive still further the comedy Austen provides in Mr. Knightley's peevish surveillance of the anagram game:

> The word was *blunder* . . . there was a blush on Jane's cheek which gave it a meaning not otherwise ostensible . . . how it all could be, was beyond his comprehension. How the delicacy, the discretion of his favourite could have been so lain asleep! He feared there must be some decided involvement. Disingenuousness and double-dealing seemed to meet him at every turn. These letters were but the vehicle for gallantry and trick. It was a child's play, chosen to conceal a deeper game on Frank Churchill's part. (p. 326)

In the tradition of conduct literature, Mr. Knightley is prepared to protect the ladies not only from a possible sexual predator, but also, comically, from a dangerous anagram. Mr. Knightley's keen occupation with reading and comprehending the word "*blunder*" is actuated by generic concerns that Austen wishes to parody.

The fact that Mr. Knightley perceives "a blush on Jane's cheek which gave [the word '*blunder'*] a meaning not otherwise ostensible" signals to him the danger Frank Churchill represents to propriety and right conduct. Like the conduct hero of a More or Edgeworth novel, Mr. Knightley arms himself to protect the honor of the ladies present. For added comic effect, Austen provides us a rare moment of free indirect discourse as we follow Mr. Knightley's comic agitation of mind:

> With great indignation did [Mr Knightley] continue to observe [Frank]; with great alarm and distrust, to observe also his two blinded companions. He saw a short word prepared for Emma, and given to her with a look sly and demure.

Here Mr. Knightley perceives the ladies, Jane and Emma, as undoubted victims. ("With great alarm and distrust . . . [he] observe[d] . . . his two blind companions"). His anxiety is further heighten when he regards Frank Churchill prepare an anagram for Emma "with a look sly and demure." In the tradition of the rake figure, Frank's "sly and demure" look betokens a sexual advance.

Austen then depicts Mr. Knightley's further alarm when he perceives Emma accept the anagram with secret pleasure:

> He saw that Emma had soon made it out, and found it highly entertaining, though it was something which she judged it proper to appear to censure; for she said, "Nonsense! For shame!" He heard Frank Churchill next say, with a glance towards Jane, "I will give it to her—shall I?"—and as clearly heard Emma opposing it with eager laughing warmth. 'No, no, you must not; you shall not indeed.' (p. 327)

Emma's "eager laughing warmth" further titillates and disgusts Mr. Knightley who strains to comprehend Frank's meaning:

> It was done however. This gallant young man, who seemed to love without feeling, and to recommend himself without complaisance, directly handed over the word to Miss Fairfax, and with a particular degree of sedate civility entreated her to study it. Mr Knightley's excessive curiosity to know what this word might be, made him seize every possible moment for darting his eye towards it, and it was not long before he saw it to be *Dixon*. (p. 327)

Frank Churchill is transformed by Mr. Knightley into a rake figure ("This gallant young man, who seemed to love without feeling, and to recommend himself without complaisance"). His own apparent secret pleasure—("Mr. Knightley's excessive curiosity to know what this word might be, made him seize every possible moment for darting his eye toward it")—subverts the traditional active power of the conduct hero. Austen's parody replaces the sanctified and active "Knight" with a prudish and passive Knightley. His role as mute spectator to Frank Churchill's apparent co-flirtation further underscores his impotence in the presence of the younger suitor. If "*blunder*" has escaped him, so has "*Dixon*."

> Jane Fairfax's perception seemed to accompany his; her comprehension was certainly more equal to the covert meaning, the superior intelligence, of those five letters so arranged. She was evidently displeased; looked up, and seeing herself watched, blushed more deeply than he had ever perceived her, and saying only, "I did not

know that proper names were allowed," pushed away the letters with even an angry spirit, and looked resolved to be engaged by no other word that could be offered. Her face was averted from those who had made the attack, and turned towards her aunt . . . She was afterwards looking for her shawl—Frank Churchill was looking also—it was growing dusk, and the room was in confusion; and how they parted, Mr Knightley could not tell.

He remained at Hartfield after all the rest, his thoughts full of what he had seen; so full, that when the candles came to assist his observations, he must—yes, he certainly must, as a friend—an anxious friend—give Emma some hint, ask her some question. He could not see her in a situation of such danger without trying to preserve her. It was his duty. (pp. 327–8)

For all of Mr. Knightley's supervision, the game is played out and he is left in the dark—literally ("the candles came to assist his observations"). His place as a protector of female virtue is comically undermined by his inability to play games, what he dismisses earlier in the scene as "mere child's play." ("Jane Fairfax's . . . comprehension was certainly more equal to the covert meaning, the superior intelligence of those five letters so arranged.") His surveillance leads to no opportunity for action and his greatest fears seem to be realized ("[Jane] blushed more deeply than he had ever perceived her"). Keen to do "his duty," and with "his thoughts full of what he had seen," he perceives "danger," but all he can muster to "to preserve [Emma]" is to "ask her some question" (p. 328).

The question is whether Emma "perfectly understand[s] the degree of acquaintance between the gentleman and lady [Frank and Jane]." Without "perfectly understanding the degree" himself, however, he is in no position to correct Emma's response, or to interfere or direct her conduct. He remains impotent and unenlightened, "staggered" by the "confidence" and "satisfaction" of Emma's response:

'Oh! you amuse me excessively. I am delighted to find that you can vouchsafe to let your imagination wander—but it will not do—very sorry to check you in your first essay—but indeed it will not do. There is no admiration between them . . . I can answer for its being so on his. I will answer for the gentleman's indifference' (p. 329)

Emma's witty response suggests just how fuddy-duddy Mr. Knightley's secret surveillance of the game must have struck the other participants. Emma expresses "delight" in Mr. Knightley demonstrating a wandering "imagination"—apparently for the first time ("your first essay")—but she "silences him" with her own correction, subverting his authoritative role as the cautioning conduct hero. By the end of the scene, Mr. Knightley is thoroughly routed. He is left very much appearing as weak and enfeebled as Mr. Woodhouse, sitting irritably before the Hartfield fire:

> He found he could not be useful, and his feelings were too much irritated for talking. That he might not be irritated into an absolute fever, by the fire which Mr Woodhouse's tender habits required almost every evening throughout the year, he soon afterwards took a hasty leave, and walked home to the coolness and solitude of Donwell Abbey. (p. 329)

Unable to interpret or intervene in the games that have just passed—"he found he could not be useful"—he beats a "hasty" retreat to "the coolness and solitude of Donwell Abbey." Austen's could not paint the picture of a more vivid defeat for her conduct hero.

This *"blunder"* game of anagrams ends with Mr. Knightley "[thinking] he saw another collection of letters anxiously pushed towards [Jane], and resolutely swept away by her unexamined" (p. 327). Perhaps it is in imagining the word behind this "collection of letters" that so incapacitates him. One can only guess Mr. Knightley's fears of what the word could be considering the subsequent "danger" from which he finds it "his duty" to "try to preserve Emma." The Austen family tradition has it that the word was *"pardon."* Such an interpretation is fitting with the sequence of the scene. Frank's *"blunder"* puzzle is meant as a kind of peace offering. The *"Dixon"* puzzle is playful ribbing. The unseen (even by the reader) anagram of *"pardon"* completes the scene's larger structure: Frank seeks *"pardon"* for his *"blunder,"* including his suggestion, first guessed by Emma, that the pianoforte is a gift from *"Dixon."*

Austen's conduct hero, however, cannot perceive the value behind Frank's *"blunder,"* nor can he understand the corrective power of Frank's playful request for *"pardon."* Mr. Knightley's own "emulation" and "rivalship" blind him to the right conduct displayed in this game by Frank Churchill. Caught in his own fiction of right conduct—his role as an embodied Gisborne—his interpretation and actions throughout the scene prove that he himself, as conduct hero, is prone to "*blunder*." His steady gaze in trying discern Jane's reaction to the puzzle is not delicate, and certainly may have added the color to her blush: "[S]eeing herself watched, [she] blushed more deeply than he had ever perceived her."

Of course, it is not a coincidence that Emma too misreads the puzzle. Frank's word "*blunder*" appears to her a suggestion of Jane Fairfax's inappropriate attachment to "*Dixon*." She is blind to Frank's "double-dealing" and "deeper game." The performance is masterful and one Austen clearly took pains to conduct. At once, Frank Churchill manages to elude the surveillance of Mr. Knightley, apologize playfully to his fiancé, and to disguise his relationship from Emma further. Austen's own "deeper game" puts the lie to the simplistic conduct codes represented by the heroes and heroines of conduct literature. Austen's design becomes clear: to understand the "complete truth" of "*courtship*" and right conduct (i.e. the value of a "*blunder*") the reader must look beyond the traditional heroes and heroines of conduct literature ("seldom can it happen that something is not a little disguised, or a little mistaken"). If Mr. Knightley is set up as the embodiment of right conduct in Austen's novel, he will also come to function as a parody of right conduct, as the "*blunder*" game suggests. And if Emma functions as heroine, she is also—purposefully—the embodiment of wrong conduct ("a heroine no one will much like but myself"). Mr. Knightley can only beat his "hasty" retreat, "confused by it all," while Emma willfully misreads yet another of the novel's puzzles. As Jane Austen confided in a letter, "[p]ictures of perfection, as you know, make me sick and wicked . . ." (*Letters*, p. 134). Austen's heroes and heroines will "*blunder*" plentifully, and Austen will take "wicked" pleasure in depicting their mistakes. In this way, Austen will embody the wisdom or right conduct in a less than "perfect" world.

One final example will complete our study of Austen's theme of conduct in *Emma* and its relationship to the tradition of conduct literature. Austen agrees with Gisborne that a young woman should choose her friends from among her social equals: "let her companions be in general neither much above her own level, nor much below it." The danger in the latter case, according to Gisborne, is that a woman may be led "to assume airs of contemptuous and domineering superiority" (p. 98). Though Austen could approve of such a sentiment in a conduct book, when she comes to dramatize the sentiment in *Emma* its truth becomes vastly complicated by the novelistic enterprise of realistic narrative. Where More and Edgeworth would subordinate their characterization to the rule—in this case, their characters would work their way toward assimilating the moral "let her companions be in general neither much above her own level, nor much below it"—Austen's narrative works the other way, expressing and then testing and complicating such conduct codes by putting them to the test of realistic characterization.

When Emma wishes to adopt her social inferior Harriet Smith as her protégée, Mr. Knightley objects to the choice on the grounds that Emma's "doctrines" lack "strength of mind" and rationality. Mr. Knightley—a surrogate Gisborne once again—states the rule in form of a question and a statement:

> "How can Emma imagine she has anything to learn herself, while Harriet is presenting such a delightful inferiority? . . . I am much mistaken if Emma's doctrines give any strength of mind, or tend at all to make a girl adapt herself rationally to the varieties of her situation in life.—They only give a little polish." (p. 37)

Here Mr. Knightley echoes the sexism and snobbishness of Gisborne ("let her companions be in general neither much above her own level, nor much below it") by imagining that Emma has nothing to learn from Harriet. By "lacking strength of mind," Emma's "doctrines" cannot assist Harriet in adapting herself "rationally" to the "varieties of her situation in life." According to Mr. Knightley's edict, Emma and Harriet's friendship can only offer unsubstantial, feminine "polish." As such, Mr. Knightley advises that the friendship constitutes wrong conduct, or a "*blunder.*"

Unlike Gisborne, however, Mr. Knightley does not express the implied code of conduct in a vacuum; rather, he states it in a conversation with Emma's former governess Mrs. Weston, who knows better. No answer is made, in part, because Mrs. Weston, who cannot be unaware that she herself has little claim to being a social equal with Emma, may, in fact, be a living example of the rule's speciousness. Mrs. Weston's good sense has helped to shape Emma's character in a positive fashion, despite the fact that Mrs. Weston is decidedly much below Emma in social equality. The conduct rule may sound well in the context of a conduct book, but in a world of complex human interaction, no such rule is advisable. The realism of Austen's domestic fiction tests the truth and falsehood of Knightley's precept in a way that no other work, particularly in the conduct novel tradition, could. The rest of Austen's *Emma* serves to overturn the implied precepts of Mr. Knightley and Gisborne. If, for Mr. Knightley, women like Emma "lack [the] strength of mind" and "rational[ity]" to practice right conduct in a relationship with one who is socially their inferior, thereby committing a blunder in contracting the friendship, the business of Austen's novel will be to demonstrate the rational advantages such a relationship holds for Emma, thereby overturning Mr. Knightley's blunder in undervaluing the value of the unequal alliances. As we noted in Austen's games of *courtship* and *blunder*, Harriet holds the key to many surprising lessons in Austen, and regarding right conduct she does the same.

In these encounters, Austen is once again making the point that her conduct hero is prone to blunders, and what is worse, that he is blind to their value. Austen asks us to regard Mr. Knightley's persistent right conduct in this context. Just as he struggles with Frank Churchill's "*blunder*" anagram, Austen invites us to scrutinize Mr. Knightley's comprehension of other "*blunders*" in the novel. Thus when Mr. Elton snubs Harriet at the Crown Ball, and Mr. Knightley comes to her rescue, Austen is doing more than demonstrating Mr. Knightley's chivalry. She is also demonstrating the way in which a blunder surprises us into re-examining accepted codes of conduct. The scene is described through Emma's perspective:

> In another moment a happier sight caught [Emma];—Mr Knightley leading Harriet to the set!—Never had she been more surprised, seldom more delighted, than at that instant. (p. 307)

Emma appears to recognize the value initiated by Mr. Elton's mistake: his blunder has the happy consequence of breaking down the social codes that separate Harriet and Mr. Knightley. Where the novel opens with Mr. Knightley considering Emma's acquaintance with her inferior, Harriet, a mistake ("How can Emma imagine she has anything to learn, while Harriet is presenting such a delightful inferiority?"), Mr. Elton's snubbing of Harriet challenges Mr. Knightley's premise: crossing social boundaries to befriend an inferior is, in fact, an example of right conduct and an opportunity for growth and instruction. Austen notes, "Never had [Emma] been more surprised, seldom more delighted, than at that instant." With the dance, Mr. Knightley begins a friendship with Harriet that is almost unthinkable at the beginning of the novel. But rather than realize the value to Mr. Elton's, and his own, blunder, Mr. Knightley becomes absorbed in pontificating against Mr. Elton's snub:

> Emma had no opportunity of speaking to Mr Knightley till after supper; but, when they were all in the ball-room again, her eyes invited him irresistibly to come to her and be thanked. He was warm in his reprobation of Mr Elton's conduct; it had been unpardonable rudeness; and Mrs Elton's looks also received the due share of censure. (p. 309)

Emma appears to expect recognition of her and Mr. Knightley's accord ("Her eyes invited him irresistibly to come to her and be thanked"). But instead of realizing the similarity between her right conduct of befriending Harriet and Mr. Knightley's in doing the same, Mr. Knightley instead grows "warm" in "reprobat[ing]" Mr. Elton's conduct. His focus does not shift to the object of his kindness (Harriet), but remains in the mode of self-righteous condemnations: "[I]t had been unpardonable rudeness; and Mrs. Elton's looks also received the due share of censure, righteously condemning the conduct of now Mrs. Elton." Clearly, the similarity between Mr. Elton's snub, and his own in regarding Harriet as a worthy friend to Emma escapes him. Once again regarding this particular anagram on "*blunder*," it is Mr. Knightley who still has the most to learn.

Those who read *Emma* as only a novel in which the heroine undergoes an education of experience in right conduct from Mr. Knightley, miss half the story, along with most of the novel's good jokes. No doubt, the logic of the novel makes some element of this reading undeniable. Mr. Knightley does assist Emma in regulating her conduct, especially as it regards her jealousy to Jane Fairfax and her snobbishness towards the Martins, the Coles, and others. But Mr. Knightley, despite his superiority of age and experience, is also lacking in right conduct himself. Early in the novel he says, "I should like to see Emma in love, and in some doubt of a return; it would do her good" (p. 39). He is quite right, but the irony, as we noted earlier, is that only when he becomes jealous of Frank Churchill does he begins to understand his own feelings. Emma is rude to Miss Bates, while flushed with the pleasure of showing off with Churchill, and gets properly corrected for it by Mr. Knightley, but he, under the pressure of jealousy, is quite rude to Miss Bates himself. Angry at seeing " 'that fellow Churchill showing off his own voice'," he says, " 'Miss Bates, are you mad, to let your niece sing herself hoarse in this manner? Go and interfere' " (p. 213). Mr. Knightley's angry rebuke of Miss Bates—warmed by jealousy of Frank Churchill—has a the potential of humiliating Miss Bates far more than Emma's clever retort during the Box Hill excursion.

Everywhere one turns in the text Mr. Knightley guides the way to right conduct, stating the precepts of proper behavior in the stately cadences of conduct literature. But, the novel and Emma—full of wit and word games—refuse to allow Mr. Knightley to remain blind to the opportunity of a blunder—his and other's. Austen and Emma will not allow Knightley to become just another "Knight" in the tradition of conduct literature. Indeed, the novel goes to some lengths to make Mr. Knightley a figure of fun, a sententious and righteous bore, as we have seen. And the comedy continues, right up to the very end of the novel, as Mr. Knightley continues to be blind to the value of a *"blunder."* Consider the close of the Emma–Knightley courtship game, after love declarations by both Emma and Mr. Knightley, when Mr. Knightley declares:

> "Mystery; Finesse—how they pervert the understanding! My Emma, does not every thing serve to prove more and more the beauty of truth and sincerity in all our dealings with each other?" (p. 417)

Plain, open speech—direct, manly exchange and interaction, according to Mr. Knightley, are the true path to "understanding." The problem is, of course, the whole novel—and Emma's appeal as the central consciousness of the book—rests on the fact that true understanding is not so simple. It is precisely because of the "Mystery" and "Finesse" that we have a story at all. Indeed the "Mystery" and "Finesse" of Mr. Knightley's misapprehension that Emma is in love with Frank Churchill leads him into making his declaration.

He had, in fact, been wholly unsuspicious of his own influence. He had followed her into the shrubbery with no idea of trying it.

He had come, in his anxiety to see how she bore Frank Churchill's engagement, with no selfish view, no view at all, but of endeavouring, if she allowed him an opportunity to sooth or to counsel her.—The rest had been the work of the moment, the immediate effect of what he heard, on his feelings . . . [I]n the momentary conquest of eagerness over judgment, [he made his declaration] . . . (p. 404)

Here the righteous Knightley follows Emma "into the shrubbery" where at "the work of the moment" and in the "conquest of eagerness over judgment," he seeks Emma's hand in marriage. In other words, stealing behind Emma and into the "shrubbery," "eagerness" gets the better of his vaunted "judgment." Thinking that Emma is heartbroken over Frank Churchill's preference for Jane Fairfax, he tries to catch Emma on the rebound. His behavior here can only be interpreted as a social "*blunder*," unbecoming the usual "Knightley-behavior" of the conduct hero. And yet we like Mr. Knightley the better for it, and indeed, he can thank this social—and for him, scandalous—"*blunder*" for the series of revelations that bring the pair to the altar.

Austen is not done in teaching her conduct hero the lesson of the value of a "*blunder*" even after his marriage. Even at the end of the novel, Austen goes to some trouble to signal Mr. Knightley still blindly probing the meaning of "*blunder*." She writes:

Mrs Weston's poultry-house was robbed one night of all her turkies—evidently by the ingenuity of man. Other poultry-yard in the neighborhood also suffered.—Pilfering was housebreaking to Mr Woodhouse's fears.—He was very uneasy; and but for the sense of his son-in-law's protection, would have been under wretched alarm every night of his life . . . The result of this distress was, that, with a much more voluntary, cheerful consent than his daughter have ever presumed to hope for at the moment, she was able to fix her wedding day . . . (p. 452–3)

No real narrative business is being conducted here, though the passage comprises the penultimate paragraph of the novel. We already know that Emma and Mr. Knightley are pledged to marry; we know, too, that Emma and Mr. Knightley have both arrived at the solution of the couple living with Mr. Woodhouse at Hartfield after the marriage—so that no great change will disturb Mr. Woodhouse's delicate health. Why the business about the "pilfered poultry"?

Surely, the effect is meant to be comic at Mr. Woodhouse's expense. But Austen, too, holds up Mr. Knightley for his share of ridicule. In what must be one of the biggest blunders in the comic novel tradition, Mr. Knightley abandons his own capacious grounds at Donwell Abbey so that he can move into the house of his invalid father-in-law to look after his chickens until Mr. Woodhouse's decease—which may be some time delayed considering the power of gruel and the keen attendance of Mr. Perry. He may well wish he were again a bachelor contemplating Frank's "*blunder*" instead of his own. At least then, he could take "a hasty leave, and walk home to the coolness and solitude of Donwell Abbey." Instead, he is likely to remain suspended in the moment in which he puzzled over that first "*blunder*" ("irritated into an absolute fever, by the fire which Mr. Woodhouse's tender habits required almost every evening through-out the year"). Only love could reduce such a stern, erect figure as Mr. Knightley into a protector of the Woodhouse chicken pen, by casting him into this peculiar living hell. ("Mystery; Finesse—how they pervert the understanding!") If Emma has already had this effect on Mr. Knightley's vaunted reason, one can only wonder where he will be lead next. Mr. Knightley's own judgment on Emma and Harriet proves particularly apt:

> How can Mr Knightley imagine he has anything to learn himself, while Mr Woodhouse is presenting such a delightful inferiority? . . . I am much mistaken if Mr Knightley's doctrines give any strength of mind, or tend at all to make a man adapt himself rationally to the varieties of his situation in life. (p. 37)

Certainly, such a conclusion subverts the gender equation that places women subordinate to men in reason.

WELLBEING

The third primary theme in *Emma* is the theme of wellbeing. The theme is the natural goal of the comedic form that Austen's *Emma* helps fashion for the English novel tradition. As we noted in Chapter 2, in a comic novel characters are fitted into the larger social order and a sense of harmony and reconciliation is achieved. Because virtue is rewarded and vice is punished, a sense of poetic justice also prevails. Thus, comedic endings offer a vision of the world as well-ordered and generally sympathetic to human needs and desires. At the end of *Emma* such wellbeing is established: the community of Highbury is regenerated as the marriages of Jane Fairfax and Frank Churchill, Emma Woodhouse and Mr. Knightley, and Harriet Smith and Robert Martin harmonize and "in spite of . . . deficiencies, the wishes, the hopes, the confidence, the predictions of the small band of true friends . . . [are] fully answered in the perfect happiness of union" (p. 453). The disapproving Eltons are left out of this wedding celebration, signaling that the other characters have closed ranks to cast them out socially, not because their marriage is any less well conceived ("Power" + "Wealth" + "luxury and ease" = "*courtship*"), but rather because their conduct in achieving and maintaining marriage is less skillful (read more *blundering*) than that of the other unions. Courtship, right conduct, and wellbeing comically triumph.

To understand Austen's conclusion fully, however, we need to consider further the final theme inherent in this comic ending: wellbeing. The prominent example of wellbeing in the novel is its namesake, Emma. Throughout the novel, Austen goes to great lengths to depict Emma's vitality of spirit and mind. Early on, we get Emma's portrait (as described by Mrs. Weston) as a kind of physical exam, or checkup:

> "Such an eye!—the true hazle eye—and so brilliant! regular features, open countenance, with a complexion! oh! what a bloom of full health, and such a pretty height and size; such a firm and upright figure. There is health, not merely in her bloom, but in her air, her head, her glance. One hears sometimes of a child being 'the picture of health;' now Emma always gives me the idea of being the complete picture of grown-up health. She is loveliness itself. Mr Knightley, is not she?" (p. 38)

The figure against which such wellbeing is emphasized is that of her father, Mr. Woodhouse, a notorious hypochondriac, who is described as "a nervous man, easily depressed." He suffers from a nervous complaint that is sketched as the sum of his character. Everything about Mr. Woodhouse works in service to his illness, mental and bodily. The result is his comic medical caution for all those about him:

"Young ladies are delicate plants. They should take care of their health and their complexion. My dear, did you change your stockings?" (p. 273)

What was unwholesome to him, he regarded as unfit for any body; and he had, therefore, earnestly tried to dissuade them from having any wedding cake at all, and when that proved vain, as earnestly tried to prevent any body's eating it. (p. 20)

As we already noted, the novel ends keeping father and daughter united: Emma and Mr. Knightley join Mr. Woodhouse at Hartfield as a way for Emma and Mr. Knightley to continue to ensure Mr. Woodhouse's wellbeing. Such a conclusion is a curious picture of the comedic ending: wellbeing is held in the service of illness. All may not be well at the end of Austen's book. Surely, the closing invites the question: what kind of "picture of health" is Austen depicting here?

One of the best books written on Austen in general, and on *Emma* in particular, is John Wiltshire's *Jane Austen and the Body: The Picture of Health* (CUP, 1992). I will be drawing liberally from Wiltshire's study as we survey the theme of wellbeing. Wiltshire argues that the novel's obsession with sickness and health has an important ethical dimension. As he puts it, "to think about health is necessarily to think morally" (p. 153). His reading of Austen's novel celebrates Emma as an active, charitable, and generous heroine whose free-flowing spirits remain unbounded in the face of her father's negative, confining tendencies associated with his mental and physical illness. We will follow Wiltshire's lead, but push further to see precisely what "picture of health" Austen intends in the closing union of Emma, Mr. Woodhouse, and Mr. Knightley.

Mr. Perry is, as Wiltshire observes, the "omnipresent and very active, but scarcely seen" attending physician of the text, cloistered with Mr. Woodhouse while the action goes on elsewhere. We glimpse Mr. Perry occasionally as he makes his rounds about the village, as when Emma catches sight of him "walking hastily by" as she is waiting outside Ford's while Harriet shops, or when he is reported on indirectly, sometimes through two or three intermediaries. The nature of such intermediating narration captures brilliantly the role of gossip as a vehicle of community in Highbury. For instance, when Harriet tells Emma how Miss Nash has told her that Mr. Perry told *her*, that he saw Mr. Elton on the road carrying Emma's portrait of Harriet—

Mr. Perry teases Mr. Elton, "He was very sure there must be a lady in the case." Here we get the gossip, and Mr. Perry's words, fifth-hand. Mr. Perry's role as a relay station for gossip captures the distinctive feel of the way a village physician acts as a conduit of information. Mr. Perry is likely to appear, as Wiltshire notes, "every twenty or thirty pages," usually implied, not present, circulating as part of the healthy function of the community (pp. 110–11). He is one of a number of examples of figures that occupy such a middle distance of the text, access to whose direct conversation or thoughts we are not privy. Many of the allusions to Mr. Perry, such as Emma's recalling for her father how Mr. Perry nursed her through the measles, serve to make his presence appear more pervasive and permanent than if he appeared in numerous scenes. The effect is one of quiet but pervasive attendance, an important intermediary attending more than any other single character, fittingly, to the theme of wellbeing in Austen's novel.

Though a professional, Mr. Perry is, like Mr. Cole and Mr. Weston, an entrepreneur, finding prosperity with his rise in reputation. The fact that he can consider buying a carriage and setting up as a gentleman suggests his constant attendance on Highbury's richest patients. When called to assist the genteel poor, like the Bates family, he does not, Austen makes clear, charge a fee—a point that further distinguishes his claim to gentlemanly status. Significantly, even Mr. Perry's social mobility, when it is discussed in the community, centers on the question of wellbeing and illness. When the prospect of his purchase of a carriage is discussed, the potential acquisition is discussed not as a sign of his prosperity, or his social prestige, but in terms of his own ill health. Frank recites the gossip thus: "It was owing to [Mrs. Perry's] persuasion, as she thought his being out in bad weather did him a great deal of harm" (p. 323). The effect is to demonstrate the primacy of health over social claims, even with Highbury's devoted physician.

In *Emma*, both the rich and the powerful, the high and the low— Mrs. Churchill of Enscombe and the poor cottager whom Emma and Harriet go to visit—are recognized as suffers of ill health. The novel holds a virtual medicine chest of para-medical talk and paraphernalia: from Harriet's treasured court-plaister, to Isabella's claims about the favorable air of Brunswick Square, to the Hartfield arrowroot dispatched for Jane, to speculation over Frank Churchill's special "constitution" that makes him cross when hot. As Wiltshire's study makes clear, these matters of health are not merely incidental concerns in the novel, rather Austen's focus on wellbeing and illness illuminates her characters in significant ways: we learn the nature of the novel's characters by observing the ways in which they react to the sickness of others, their degree of forbearance and the kindnesses they show or omit (p. 112).

A set of examples will assist. It is fitting that Frank Churchill shows solicitude for the deaf and nearly blind Mrs. Bates by fixing her spectacles. He at once demonstrates a kind impulse (assisting Mrs. Bates with her failing eyesight) while also using the repair as an opportunity to dally with Jane by the piano—both correcting vision and blinding at once. One would expect nothing less from the novel's hero of "double-dealing." Equally illuminating is the more sympathetic portrait of Miss Bates that is revealed if we attend to her care for the ill instead of judging her for her garrulous insipidness. Austen puts such discrete medicine into the capsules of Miss Bates's free-associative disclosures that many readers fail to absorb the insight. Detailing the evening of the Box Hill excursion, when Frank has broken with Jane and returned to Richmond, Miss Bates explains:

> "It was before tea—stay—no, it could not be before tea, because we were just going to cards—and yet it was before tea, because I remember thinking—Oh! no, now I recollect, now I have it: something happened before tea, but not that. Mr Elton was called out of the room before tea, old John Abdy's son wanted to speak with him. Poor old John, I have a great regard for him; he was clerk to my poor father twenty-seven years; and now, poor old man, he is bed-ridden, and very poorly with the rheumatic gout in his joints—I must go see him today; and so will Jane, I am sure, if she gets out at all. And poor John's son came to talk to Mr Elton about relief from the parish; he is very well to do himself, you know, being head man at the Crown, ostler, and every thing of that sort, but still he cannot keep his father without some help; and so, when Mr Elton came back, he told us what John ostler had been telling him, and then it came out about the chaise having been sent to Randall's to take Mr Frank Churchill to Richmond. That was what happened before tea. It was after tea that Jane spoke to Mrs Elton." (pp. 358–9)

The beauty of Austen's art can be found in this set of free-associations from Miss Bates. Released amid Miss Bates's dynamic chatter is information that explains why Jane has suddenly decided to take the job as governess. However, if the reader views Miss Bates only from perspective of seeking immediate plot disclosure, the reader may agree with Emma that there is "nothing in all this either to astonish or interest." Emma already knows that Frank has returned to Richmond, though she remains unaware of the nature of his departure and of the now broken engagement—details released here to the attentive reader, but not taken in by Emma. These such would likely astonish, if Emma were perceptive enough to attend. But more information is released than even this: Miss Bates is revealed as a kind, attentive, and thoughtful human being, attending to the needs and cares of such a one as "poor John Aby," the former clerk to her father. There is something medicinal and fortifying in the way Austen depicts the virtuous actions of such unpretending characters as Miss Bates. Virtue in the novel is not always announced in the sententious cadences of Mr. Knightley; sometimes virtue is incidental, unpremeditated, even a little silly, as it is with the much-lambasted Miss Bates (Wiltshire 1986, p. 114).

Mr. Perry, as attending physician to this text, has his hands full—and he needs all the assistance he can get from the Miss Bateses of Highbury. The textual infirmary of the novel overflows. Every major character is threatened by, or undergoes, an illness during the course of the book—Emma, Jane Fairfax, Mrs. Elton, and so on—even Mr. Knightley suffers the onset of the fever that he narrowly escapes with his "hasty" retreat to "the coolness and solitude of Donwell Abbey," as we noted earlier. Isabella Knightley complains of "those little nervous head-aches and palpitations which I am never entirely free from any where" (p. 99); Harriet experiences a serious attack of what is likely the flu (Chapters 14 and 15), leading to Mr. Elton's tête-à-tête with Emma (p. 122); Mrs. Weston and Jane Fairfax join many others in an epidemic outbreak of "nervous disorder" that lays so many low at one point or another. The two grand embodiments of both illness in general, and "nervous disorder" in particular, are Mr. Woodhouse and Mrs. Churchill. The pair are significant to our concern because both also embody a direct threat to Austen's comic ending. The successful outcome of courtship, conduct, and wellbeing uniting the novels three sets of married couples could not be accomplished without the demise of Mrs. Churchill and the acceptance of Mr. Woodhouse. Wellbeing at the end of the novel is intimately tied up to the medical fate of the work's two most ill characters, as we will see.

Once again we turn to the work of John Wiltshire and his scholarship clarifying the medical context of many of the illnesses per-
vading Austen's text. Nervous disorder, as Wiltshire documents, was
a common diagnosis in this period. Wiltshire offers historical details
that explain the context, including Fanny Burney's court journal,
work by the medical historian W. F. Bynum, George Cheyne's
popular 1733 medical treatise, Robert Whytt's mid-eighteenth
investigations on the nervous system, and Dr. Thomas Trotter's 1807
book *A View of the Nervous Temperament*. Fanny Burney's journal
reports in 1788 that the King himself was a suffer of the
Woodhouse–Churchill complaint: " 'I am nervous' he cried; 'I am
not ill, but I am nervous; if you would know what is the matter with
me, I am nervous.' " W. F. Bynum observes: "It was . . . only in the
eighteenth century that it became possible to suffer from the
'nerves.' " The notion of the nerves and the nervous system as a
source of human suffering is popularized by Cheyne's textbook. In
the textbook, Cheyne describes the nervous patient as "a personality type found in those with 'weak, loose, and feeble, or relaxed
nerves,' the result of which was extreme sensitivity to hot and cold,
weak digestion, a tendency to alternative diarrhoea and costiveness,
and other signs of valetudinarianism." Cheyne further observes that
"Nervous disorders are the Diseases of the Wealthy, the Voluptuous
and the Lazy." The argument of his book is that "Nervous disorders" are the product of increasing wealth and leisure among the
middle classes, an argument widely accepted and adopted among
medical textbooks into the nineteenth century. Robert Whytt's
medical work exploring irritability, sensibility, and the nervous
system is pioneering in the period for grafting the new "scientific"
understanding propagated by Cheyne onto the amplified sensibility
that he attributed to the leisure classes. For Whytt, as you move
beyond the middle classes and into the leisure classes, you find
further nervous disorders associated with the "the Wealthy, the
Voluptuous and the Lazy" (Wiltshire 1986, p. 117).

Dr. Thomas Trotter's 1807 treatise, *A View of the Nervous
Temperament*, as Wiltshire notes, provides a telling diagnosis of
aspects relative to the conditions of Mr. Woodhouse and Mrs.
Churchill as described in *Emma*:

An inaptitude to muscular action, or some pain in exerting it; an
irksomeness, or dislike to attend to business and the common

affairs of others to the narration of their own sufferings; with fickleness and unsteadiness of temper, even to irascibility: and accompanied more of less with dyspeptic symptoms, are the leading characteristics of nervous disorders; to be referred in general, to debility, increased sensibility, or torpor of the alimentary canal. (Qtd in 1986, p. 118)

The social profile Trotter provides to accompany this diagnosis is equally apposite with our understanding of Mr. Woodhouse and Mrs. Churchill's financial standings. For Trotter, "torpid habits of living" are the consequence of patients with money earning compound interest and having no need to work for their livelihood, "without any of those urgent motives which preserve energy of mind, so condusive [sic] to health." Trotter goes on to characterize a relationship that echoes uncannily that of Mr. Woodhouse and his reliance on Mr. Perry

Being singular in the selection of friends, they seldom mix in company; sedentary from habit, they go little abroad; their amusements and recreation are thus limited, and such as possess the talent of bringing news, and telling a story, are at all times welcome guests. But as the tale of their own complaints engrosses so much of their conversation, a medical gossip, before all others, is the most acceptable. (Qtd in Wilshire 1986, p. 118)

The recommended treatment for the symptoms of nervous disorder diagnosed in Cheyne, Trotter, and other physicians emphasize a frugal diet, exercise, and fresh air. For instance, in the case of young ladies, gardening and walking are recommended: "And while her nervous aunts are moping their evenings over the card table, she will gather health by her cheerful excursions; and preserve her bloom of countenance by the only means that can give it an additional charm" (qtd in Wiltshire 1986, p. 119). The medical advice parallels Austen's narrator in commending Mrs. Goddard's school in Highbury, "reckoned a particularly healthy spot" where Mrs. Goddard lets the students "run about a great deal in summer, and in winter dressed their chilblains with her own hands." Significantly, Harriet Smith, a product of such medically advisable practices, is one of the few women in Highbury that escape a "nervous complaint"—despite three or four near/broken engagements. Presumably, at more affluent and prestigious schools, "nervous complaints" are more prevalent, where, as the narrator observes, the girls are "screwed out of health and into vanity" (pp. 22–3, qtd in Wiltshire 1986, p. 119)

Trotter's diagnosis at times comes to parallel Mr. Woodhouse's solicitude for the other characters in Austen's text, especially Jane Fairfax. Trotter's discussion of wet feet among ladies echoes Mr. Woodhouse's alarm over Jane Fairfax's stocking noted earlier:

> The lady of weak health, who may wish to display an ancle [sic], should be very guarded how she throws off her warm socks. Many evils befall [sic] the sex from cold feet: such as follow on walking abroad with thin shoes on damp roads . . . I have known some serious nervous ailments brought on by a young lady evading the orders of a judicious parent; and after being dressed, retiring privately to put off the additional petticoat and understockings, that she might dance more lightly. (Qtd in Wiltshire 119)

Here "medical" advice is clearly shaped by gender politics and ideology, as Wiltshire correctly notes. A young lady is defined equally by her propensity to sickness ("lady of weak health . . . many evils befall [sic] the sex") and coquettishness ("wish to display an ancle [sic]" and "putting off the additional petticoat and understockings, that she might dance more lightly"). The authority of the physician and the authority of the male supervisor coalesce ("I have known . . ." and "evading the orders of a judicious parent"). Trotter's "medical" science, in this case, comes to resemble Mr. Woodhouse's "nervous illness." In the scene where Mr. Woodhouse cautions Jane Fairfax about a "wet stocking," he also assures Miss Fairfax: "My dear, young ladies are very sure to be cared for." Both Trotter and Mr. Woodhouse position women, given their gender, as patients, or potential patients. Both consider women to be entitled to "care," but a "care" that puts them under the constant surveillance of a "judicious parent," or patriarchal authority.

The games of courtship and the theme of conduct that we have explored so far are incomplete without taking into account the well-being and illness of Mr. Woodhouse and Mrs. Churchill. Courtship and conduct are inextricably linked to these powerful figures who similarly control aspects of the plot through the manipulation of their illnesses in association with their control over wealth and the spoils of inheritance. Their illnesses are real; the richly documented work of

Wiltshire clearly places the pair as not simply willful hypochondriacs. Indeed, Mrs. Churchill's surprising demise in the face of her perceived fake illnesses makes the point emphatically. Still, the "willful" sides of their disorders provide Mr. Woodhouse and Mrs. Churchill unequal latitude as blocking elements to the novel's comedic form. Mrs. Churchill, who is described as suffering from "nerves," operates in the novel as the covert double of Mr. Woodhouse, the "nervous man." While Emma spends much energy and time attending to and comforting her father, Frank Churchill does the same as the adopted son of Mrs. Churchill. Both characters, elderly and rich, hold the power of preventing the marriage of their favorites. If Mrs. Churchill uses her illnesses to keep Frank at home and to prevent him from marrying, by fear that he will displease her and be disinherited, Mr. Woodhouse similarly practices control over Emma using his ill health to confine her at home and to discourage the social contacts and journeys abroad that might lead to her marriage.

In this light the figures of Emma, and especially Frank Churchill, become more sympathetic. Frank Churchill's "double-dealing" and duplicity are more pardonable when you take into account his relationship with Mrs. Churchill. As an adopted son and Mrs. Churchill's favorite, his engagement to Jane Fairfax—which resembles her sister's marriage to Captain Weston, an unsuitably low connection—must be kept secret or he would be "thrown off with due decorum." Perhaps because there is a strong resemblance in their predicaments, Emma discernibly interprets Frank's relationship with Mrs. Churchill:

> His importance at Enscombe was very evident. He did not boast, but it naturally betrayed itself, that he had persuaded his aunt where his uncle could do nothing, and on her laughing and noticing it, he owned that he believed (excepting one or two points) he could *with time* persuade her to anything" (p. 206)

The "one or two points" no doubt includes his engagement with the penniless Jane. At this point in the text, February, Frank has been engaged for almost six months, and presumably he is playing for time to bring his aunt around—no easy task, at least if Mrs. Churchill resembles the "nervous" and disagreeable woman that she is represented as by all witnesses in the tale. To succeed, he will need all his charm—charm that Frank sharpens daily in his interactions among the Highbury set. And so, just as preparations are underway for the Crown Ball and Frank is nearing the long delayed opportunity to dance again with Jane Fairfax, Mrs. Churchill summons him. And he must go.

> A letter arrived from Mr Churchill to urge his nephew's instant return. Mrs Churchill was unwell—far too unwell to do without him; she had been in a very suffering state (so said her husband) when writing to her nephew two days before, though from her usual unwillingness to give pain, and constant habit of never thinking of herself, she had not mentioned it; but now she was too ill to trifle, and must entreat him to set off for Enscombe without delay. (p. 240)

This summons is just one of many that he dutifully attends. Frank is prevented from making the strawberry party, too, by "a temporary increase of illness in her; a nervous seizure, which had lasted some hours" (p. 341). Here, Wiltshire's interpretation is too precise not to quote at length:

> Mrs Churchill then, has great—in fact, very precise and crucial—influence upon the action of the novel. Without her, there would be no need to keep the engagement so long a secret; without her illness Frank would be free to come and go, and enjoy himself as he pleases. Without her caprices he could himself be less 'self-willed' and have no need to flirt with Emma. Her demand for attention originates a cascade of incidents, for his late arrival at Donwell provokes the crisis in Frank and Jane's relationship, generating the tense and unhappy Box Hill party, which in turn impacts upon Emma and her relationship with Mr Knightley. She is thus the always absent origin of the novel's events. High in social hierarchy, she is high in the hierarchy of causes. Her power—based, of course, on her status as an elder and her affluence—infiltrates the smallest events of provincial Highbury. (pp. 122–3)

Mrs. Churchill exerts a surprising power over the shape of the novel as Wiltshire's extended analysis brilliantly details. But what, then, of her surprising demise? Wiltshire's interest does not extend to this, but it must now occupy us. How does Mrs. Churchill's death fit in with the novel's concluding "picture of health" in the union of courtship, conduct, and wellbeing? In other words, why does Austen kill her off so unceremoniously?

Certainly, a simple answer would be that Austen wanted to close down her comic novel and hand out just desserts. It was easier to kill off Mrs. Churchill to clear the way for Frank and Jane than to find another way of removing her influence. But if Austen was so concerned in creating an unambiguous comedic ending, she could have just as easily killed off the feeble Mr. Woodhouse—there would have been a kind of symmetry in disposing of the two embodied illnesses blocking the comic resolution of her story. Implicit in Mrs. Churchill's demise is something of the medical diagnosis Wiltshire helps us recover: she represents the sickness of the "Wealthy, the Voluptuous and the Lazy." She embodies "the leisure classes" whose amplified sensibility is wrongly indulged. Mrs. Churchill's "nervousness" extends out from her own bodily and mental illness and comes to infect the unsettled nature of the novel's various games of courtship. The Jane Fairfax–Frank Churchill romance is not a healthy affair, and the secrecy and evasiveness that the two must practice due to her influence begins to sicken and threaten their union. The portrait of their deteriorating relationship can be glimpsed in the increasing hopelessness by which Jane prepares to give herself up to becoming a governess, with no concern for the specifics of the circumstance. Like an attending physician, then, Austen closes the door quickly on Mrs. Churchill (her bodily remains disappear unnoticed in the text)—Austen's narrative sleight-of-hand provides the restorative draught that saves Frank Churchill, and especially Jane Fairfax, from the brink of disaster. The swiftness by which Mrs. Churchill's influence is shunted aside, and her views and wishes are discarded, suggests Austen's ironic judgment against Mrs. Churchill's sick influence, more imaginary than real, but not the less powerful. The social codes and laws that enable Mrs. Churchill to conduct the course of the novel are in need of comic redress. By exposing the illness of Mrs. Churchill's imaginary power and its quick dissipation from the text, Austen suggests a revolutionary politics usually not apprehended in her work: as the embodiment of the "Wealthy, the Voluptuous and the Lazy," Mrs. Churchill represents a mental illness that can only be addressed by its bodily demise.

Mr. Woodhouse is a different matter. The logic of the novel's various games of courtship, conduct, and wellbeing find no need to dispense with him. Apparently, his illness, unlike Mrs. Churchill's, does not need to be cast out for Austen's comic purpose. Indeed, the novel goes to some trouble to close with his illness being recognized, accepted, and coddled. As we have noted, Austen's comedic ending is a strange one with the hero and heroine living in a kind of suspended animation administering to Mr. Woodhouse's wellbeing. Perhaps the strangest quality of Austen's *Emma* is the way the novel itself (including its readers) are ultimately drawn back at its close into the role of the unseen but ever present Mr. Perry, attending to the needs, fears, and wishes of Mr. Woodhouse. If Mrs. Churchill is killed off because she represents the sickness of the "Voluptuous and the Lazy," of "the leisure classes" whose amplified sensibility is wrongly indulged—why does Mr. Woodhouse become a part of the "unity" expressed in the novel's close?

Again Austen's theme here is drawn out as part of the novel's social games and word puzzles. If the theme of wellbeing is initiated in the sharp distinction between the characterization of Mr. Woodhouse—slow, sickly, cautious—and Emma—witty, vibrant, prone to adventure—the theme finds its playful incarnation in Mr. Woodhouse's contribution to Harriet's riddle book. The circumstances and details of Mr. Woodhouse's contribution to the puzzle book is worth recounting in full. In helping Harriet prepare her book of charades, Emma asks her father if he has any riddles or puzzles that they might include. The question becomes a preoccupation for the sickly Mr. Woodhouse as he tries to remember riddles from his youth:

> Mr Woodhouse was almost as much interested in the business as the girls, and tried very often to recollect something worth putting in. "So many clever riddles there used to be when he was young— he wondered he could not remember them! but he hoped he should in time." And it always ended in "Kitty, a fair but frozen maid." (p. 68)

Austen's audience would have known precisely the riddle Mr. Woodhouse was trying to recall. Attributed to the widely popular actor and producer David Garrick (1717–79), the riddle "Kitty, a fair but frozen maid" first appeared in Part Four (1771) of the printer John Almon's six-part miscellany, *New Foundling Hospital for Wit*. Garrick's riddle, like Almon's collected miscellany, is a veritable catalogue of bawdy jokes and puzzles. The riddles runs thus:

A RIDDLE
BY THE SAME, [i. e. By MR GARRICK.]

Kitty, a fair but frozen maid,
Kindled a flame I still deplore;
The hood-winked boy I call'd in aid,
Much of his near approach afraid,
So fatal to my suit before.

At length, propitious to my pray'r,
The little urchin came;
At once he fought the midway air,
And soon he clear'd, with dextrous care,

The bitter relics of my flame.
To Kitty, Fanny now succeeds,
She kindles slow, but lasting fires:
With care my appetite she feeds;
Each day some willing victim bleeds,
To satisfy my strange desires.

Say, by what title or what name,
Must I this youth address?
Cupid and he are not the same,
Though both can raise, or quench a flame –
I'll kiss you if you guess.

The fact that the riddle's prize is a "kiss . . . if [you] guess" suggests its relationship to the riddle of "*courtship*" earlier. The nature of the puzzle's darker allusions point more directly to the novel's theme of conduct and its exploration of blunders.

The benign reading of the riddle holds the answer "chimney sweep." "Kitty, the fair but frozen maid" designates a frozen piece of wood: the "Kindled . . . flame [the riddler] still deplore[s]" is the unsuccessful fire and unspent wood resulting from a clogged chimney. The "propitious [answer] to my pray'r" is the call of the chimney sweep ("the little urchin came; / At once he fought the midway air"). The sweep proves successful ("soon he clear'd, with dextrous care, / The bitter relics of my flame"). A second piece of wood is produced ("To Kitty, Fanny now succeeds") and it proves successful ("She kindles slow, but lasting fires"). Subsequent woods also works as fuel ("With care my appetite she feeds; / Each day some willing victim bleeds, / To satisfy my strange desires"). The query to the riddle's auditor challenges the identification of "The hood-winked boy I call'd in aid" from the first stanza and the "little urchin" in the second. The hint announced at the puzzle's close makes a distinction between the answer to the puzzle and Cupid ("Cupid and he are not the same, / Though both can raise, or quench a flame—I'll kiss you if you guess').

If that were all that were to the riddle, Austen's readers, like Mr. Woodhouse, would have difficulty recalling the puzzle. But the riddle was famous as a bawdy gentleman's joke regarding prostitution, syphilis, and the conquest of virgins, and its surprising appearance among so many other significant puzzles invites scrutiny. The fact that this contribution to Harriet's riddle book has been omitted and overlooked for nearly 200 years of commentary, until Jillian Heydt-Stevenson's 2005 study, suggests how much critics have resembled Mr. Woodhouse in their repressive efforts at recalling Austen's text.

The more common and bawdy reading of the puzzle recounts the riddler's contracting syphilis ("a flame I yet deplore") from a prostitute, Kitty ("Kitty" was widely used as slang for prostitute). The second stanza describes a painful method of curing syphilis involving catheterizing the penis ("And soon he clear'd, with dextrous care, / The bitter relics of my flame"). The speaker maintains in the third stanza that from now on he will only have sex with a virginal Fanny ("Fanny" was a slang word for vagina)—"Each day some willing victim bleeds / To satisfy my strange desires." The "strange desire" for a "willing victim [to] bleed" denotes the medical belief that sex with virgins cured syphilis by helping to extinguish its "flame." In this context, the puzzle's end is particularly salacious:

> Say, by what title or what name,
> Must I this youth address?
> Cupid and he are not the same,
> Though both can raise, or quench a flame –
> I'll kiss you if you guess.

The hint to the puzzle signals that "Cupid" and the traditional mythologies of love have little to do with the "rais[ing], or quench[ing]" of this puzzle's "flame." The "flame" denotes at once the burning symptom of syphilis, unquenchable desire, and the "raise" embodied in male sexual arousal. The riddle's innocent solution, "a chimney sweep," and its prize, "a kiss" are slang expressions for sexual intercourse. The literal answer to the riddle "chimney sweep" regards a woman as a "youth" whose virginal status both simultaneously quenches the flame of male sexual desire while also providing a cleansing of the male penis, a cleansing more gentle than the catheterization alluded to in the second stanza. The "name" by which the gentleman addresses "this youth" is at once "chimney sweep," "prostitute," "virgin," and "whore."

Potent stuff indeed to be recalled for inclusion in Harriet's riddle book, the companion piece to Mr. Elton's "*courtship*" puzzle! The repressed nature of Mr. Woodhouse's riddle suggests that he may be sicker than he is generally acknowledged. At least that is the interpretation of Heydt-Stevenson who first brought the history of this missing puzzle to light. Her brilliant diagnosis is worth quoting in length:

> Through a series of covert allusions, Austen raises the ludicrous and hilarious possibility that the clearly asexual Mr Woodhouse might have been a libertine in his youth and now suffers from tertiary syphilis. For example, Emma's father, a hypochondriac, cannot bear to be cold and so prefers a fire, even in midsummer; the riddle's narrator, ill with venereal disease, also longs for fire to cure him. Both Mr Woodhouse and the narrator despise marriage and want to surround themselves with young virgins who will keep them 'well.' Further, it is also deliciously, though seditiously, funny that one of the repeated cures for venereal disease was a light diet mostly consisting of a thin gruel—Mr Woodhouse's favourite meal, and the only one he can 'with thorough self-approbation, recommend.' (p. 320)

Heydt-Stevenson probably overreaches with this analysis. As we have already seen, the most likely cause of Mr. Woodhouse's illness is his "nervous complaint" fitting with the medical literature of Austen's day. Still, the fact that Austen clearly gestures to the possibilities Heydt-Stevenson uncovers suggests Austen's willingness to invite a darker interpretation of Mr. Woodhouse than most readers commonly hold.

But still the question remains: what does the self-repressed, possibly syphilitic Mr. Woodhouse have to do with the "picture of health" and wellbeing Austen appears to be painting at the close of *Emma*? Such a puzzle remains more elusive than the puzzle of Henry Woodhouse's sexual perversity. Likely, Austen, who was sickened by "pictures of perfection" ("[p]ictures of perfection, as you know, make me sick and wicked" (p. 335)) found a type of "wicked" fun in marrying Mr. Woodhouse to the fates of her hero and heroine. After all, Emma's appeal as "the picture of health" in the novel comes from the vitality she exhibits in at once honoring and loving her father, while subverting his will. The wellbeing that Emma embodies throughout the text is partly defined, as is the case with all the characters in the text, by her charitable response to the needs of others. If Emma's snobbishness and jealousy demonstrate against her character throughout the novel, her constant care and attention for her father (while exerting her own vivacious will over his) is the mark of both her moral character and her continued vital appeal to modern readers.

The parable of Mrs. Weston's wedding cake early in the text provides a suggestive vision of the comedic "unity" Austen has in mind by bringing courtship, conduct, and wellbeing together in the marriage of Emma, Mr. Knightley, and Mr. Woodhouse at the novel's close. This comic episode at the end of Chapter 2 is illustrative of Austen's closing design:

> What was unwholesome to him, he regarded as unfit for any body; and he had, therefore, earnestly tried to dissuade them from having any wedding cake at all, and when that proved vain, as earnestly tried to prevent any body's eating it. He had been at the pains of consulting Mr Perry, the apothecary, on the subject. Mr Perry was an intelligent, gentlemanlike man, whose frequent visits were one of the comforts of Mr Woodhouse's life; and, upon being applied to, he could not but acknowledge, (though it seemed rather against the bias of inclination) that wedding-cake might certainly disagree with many—perhaps with most people, unless taken moderately. With such an opinion, in confirmation of his own, Mr Woodhouse hoped to influence every visitor of the new-married pair; but still the cake was eaten; and there was no rest for his benevolent nerves till it was gone.

> There was a strange rumour in Highbury of all the little Perrys being seen with a slice of Mrs Weston's wedding cake in their hands: but Mr Woodhouse would never believe it. (p. 20)

Mrs. Weston's cake, like all wedding cakes, is a symbol of celebration and festivity. As a sensual model of the physical delights honored in marriage, the cake betokens pleasure, appetite, and generation. A wedding cake is to be eaten, and eaten with relish, a fact that clearly troubles Mr. Woodhouse, whose whole mode of life is to reduce bodily enjoyments. ("[He] earnestly tried to dissuade them from having any wedding cake at all, and when that proved vain, as earnestly tried to prevent any body's eating it.") The eating of wedding cake joins a long list of prohibited activities that Mr. Woodhouse attempts to curtail among his neighbors: walks, outings, late nights, dances, trips, expeditions, excursions, engagements, and marriage. Such activities are, he reasons, dangerous to wellbeing. His programme is the denial of almost all bodily activity, especially when pleasure may be the result—amusingly illustrated in the Woodhouse diet regimen: if one eats pork, it is to be "very thoroughly boiled, just as Serle boils our's, and eaten very moderately of, with a boiled turnip" (p. 162) (not roasted with apples as the Bateses do); if one eats tart it must be "a *little* bit of tart, a *very* little bit." Even gruel is to be concocted "thin": "Such another small basin of thin gruel as his own was all that he could, with thorough self-approbation, recommend . . ." (p. 25).

Significantly, Emma finds a way to respect and honor these peculiar requests, while also taking pleasure in practicing every one of them. Emma does not eat gruel, or "very thoroughly boiled [pork] . . . with a boiled turnip," rather she eats cake and tarts, and she takes active part in all of the novel's walks, outings, late nights, dances, trips, expeditions, excursions, engagements, and, ultimately, she even marries. Mr. Woodhouse's self-abnegating principles are defeated every time by Emma's more vital and active powers—tidily summed up in Mr. Woodhouse's recommendation to Miss Bates of "a *little* bit of tart, a *very* little bit," whereby Emma "allowed her father to talk, but supplied her visitors in a much more satisfactory style" (p. 25). And so it is that Mrs. Weston's wedding cake is also made, and eaten, and enjoyed by the community of Highbury through the agency of the novel's heroine. Away from the gaze of even the novel's narrator, Emma removes the remaining pieces of cake from beneath the notice of her father ("there was no rest for his benevolent nerves till it was gone . . .") and she secretes the pieces so that Mr. Perry can bring them home as treats for his children, at once allaying Mr. Woodhouse's anxieties, while also affirming the vitality associated with appetite and comic pleasure: "There was a strange rumour in Highbury of all the little Perrys being seen with a slice of Mrs. Weston's wedding cake in their hands." The "true liberality of mind" that directs Emma to this conduct is the true source of her wellbeing. Here is "the complete picture of grown-up health . . . loveliness itself" that Mrs. Weston draws the reader's attention to in Emma.

Although feeble and presented as a comic figure, Mr. Woodhouse still represents a threat at the end of the novel: a threat to Emma's agency and a threat to the vital pleasures associated with the comic tradition such as appetite, pleasure, and generation. In a way, he embodies the death principle itself with its abnegation of everything bodily and vital, whether or not Mr. Woodhouse literally is a syphilitic libertine, as the chimney sweep puzzle suggests. By uniting her heroine and hero to Mr. Woodhouse at the end of *Emma*, Austen reaffirms her faith, not just in Emma's conquering vitality and wellbeing, but in the vitality and wellbeing of the comic tradition itself. We can close the book sure that, even with Mr. Knightley and Mr. Woodhouse in the house, Emma will see to it that she has her cake and eats it too.

Through Austen's astonishing series of courtship puzzles and conduct games, Austen produces one of the most playful and comic novels of the nineteenth century, while helping to transform the conduct novel into the high art of the realistic novel. Austen is likely telegraphing the self-consciousness by which she has prepared all of these games and puzzles when, at the Box Hill outing, she has Mr. Weston quip: "What two letters of the alphabet are there that express perfection? . . . I will tell you.—M and A—Em– ma—Do you understand?" (p. 348).

DISCUSSION POINTS, QUESTIONS, AND SUGGESTIONS FOR FURTHER STUDY

Courtship

1. Take your favorite board game—*Monopoly, Life, Snakes and Ladders*, or *Sorry!*—and unpack the pieces. Now adapt the

conventions and rules of the game to recreate the courtship games of Emma's paired couples: Robert Martin and Harriet Smith, Mr. Elton and Emma, Harriet and Mr. Elton, Frank Churchill and Jane Fairfax, Frank Churchill and Emma, Mr. Elton and Miss Hawkins, and Mr. Knightley and Emma. Rework and reconceive the game pieces, dice, spinners, cards and native rules of your game so that the game now resembles a retelling of Austen's tale. When your group is finished, your new game should be playable and fun! (Three to four students per group recommended)

2. Study closely Mr. Elton's *"courtship"* riddle, as well as the analysis this chapter provides of the riddle. Now write a *"courtship"* riddle as you conceive Emma would have written one. Then write a *"courtship"* riddle as you conceive Harriet would have written one. These riddles should then be shared with the class as a way to discuss the key terms surround the games of courtship in Austen's *Emma*.

Conduct

1. Browse and read selections from Hannah More's conduct novel, *Coelebs in Search of a Wife* (1809) and Maria Edgeworth's *Patronage* (1814). Choose two passages from More's novel and two passages from Edgeworth's. Now compare and contrast the language, dialogue, and conduct of the characters in your selected passages to the language, dialogue, and conduct of the characters in Austen's *Emma*.

2. Divide into groups of three to four students. Each group must choose one of the novel's characters: Emma, Mr. Knightley, Mr. Woodhouse, Mrs Churchill, Mr. Weston, Mrs Weston, Harriet Smith, Frank Churchill, Mr. Elton, or Mrs Elton. Drawing from direct evidence in Austen's novel your group is responsible for creating a pocket conduct book written in the persona of your chosen character. Your conduct book should be composed of no less than ten conduct rules developed by your character. Be sure to decorate your book in keeping with your character's persona.

Wellbeing

1. You are Mr. Perry. A fellow physician is interested in your attendance on Mr. Woodhouse and has asked for medical notes

concerning his condition. Write up an analysis of what you believe to be wrong with Mr. Woodhouse as well as your prescription for his improved wellbeing.

2. Austen's greatest skill as a novelist rests in her irony, her ability to give voice to a narrative that will at once affirm and challenge the characters it describes, celebrates, and condemns. Write an essay exploring the ways in which irony functions in the novel to teach moral lessons about power, admiration, responsibility, jealousy, tenderness, and good will.

Useful research might include:

- Davies, J. M. Q. "*Emma* as Charade and the Education of the Reader," *Philological Quarterly* 65 (1986): pp. 231–2.
- Litvak, Joseph, "Reading Characters: Self, Society, and Text in *Emma*," *PMLA* 100 (1985): pp. 763–73.
- Minma, Shinobu, "Self-Deception and Superiority Complex: Derangement of Hierarchy in Jane Austen's Emma," *Eighteenth-Century Fiction* 14 (2001): pp. 49–65.
- Preus, Nicholas E., "Sexuality in Emma: A Case History," *Studies in the Novel* 23 (1991): pp. 96–216.
- Rosmarin, Adena, " 'Misreading' *Emma*: The Powers and Perfidies of Interpretive History," *ELH* 51 (1984): pp. 315–42.

CHAPTER 4

CRITICAL RECEPTION AND PUBLISHING HISTORY

CRITICAL RECEPTION

Jane Austen's first and most immediate audience was the family with whom she would share her work after composing it. Indeed, her first surviving writings were addressed to her parents—a series of short plays for her father and an epistolary tale for her mother. She cared deeply about how those near her responded to her work. Her works were shared among family and friends—her sole audience until the publication of *Sense and Sensibility* in 1811. Because of Austen's awareness of an immediate audience—she often read her work aloud—she developed an uncanny ear for the measure of comedy and the ability to develop deeply satisfying plots that pleased auditors at the tale's close.

And so it should be no surprise that once Austen's work began to appear in print, she began keeping a detailed journal of "Opinions" to record the personal likes and dislikes of her immediate circle of readers. The care with which Austen recorded the reception of her work by family and friends demonstrates her awareness of the varied reception her work received. The journal of "Opinions" also shows in Austen a writer willing to take seriously the criticisms and praise of her audience. Only a writer with such a keen sense of audience could write such deeply satisfying novels.

Emma was received by Austen's friends and families with much appreciation and with some discrimination. The following are a selection of the opening entries in the journal of "Opinions" for *Emma*, consisting of responses from her brother Frank (Captain Austen), the former governess to her niece (Miss Sharp), and her favorite niece (Fanny Knight):

Captain Austen.—liked it extremely, observing that though there might be more Wit in P. & P. [Pride and Prejudice]— & an higher Morality in M. P. [Mansfield Park]—yet altogether, on account of it's peculiar air of Nature throughout, he preferred it to either.

Miss Sharp—better than M.P.—but not so well as P. & P.— pleased with the Heroine for her Originality, delighted with Mr. K. [Mr. Knightley]

Fanny K.—not so well as either P. & P. or M. P.—could not bear Emma herself.—Mr. Knightley delightful.—Should like J. F. [Jane Fairfax]—if she knew more of her.—

These immediate and early responses to *Emma* were likely valuable support for Austen in assessing her own design for the book. Frank Austen's response, the one that leads off Austen's journal, indeed, corresponds to the conscious design of the work—and Austen's own view of her accomplishment. Somewhere between the "Wit" of *Pride and Prejudice* and the discernable "higher Morality" of *Mansfield Park*, *Emma* was a work in which Austen attempted to bring together "Wit" and "higher Morality" to create a more complex vision of the comedy of manners than she had accomplished in the earlier works.

For all the solid recognition and attention Austen's *Emma* received by contemporaries, the work, and Austen's reputation, was slow in gaining the high status they have enjoyed in the twentieth and early twenty-first centuries. Indeed, even *Emma*, Austen's most highly regarded work in her day and ours, had its detractors among her contemporaries. The novelist Maria Edgeworth, to whom Austen had sent a complimentary copy, could only make her way through the first of the works three volumes. She notes:

There was no story in it, except that Miss Emma found that the man whom she designed for Harriet's lover was an admirer of her own—& he was affronted at being refused by Emma & Harriet wore the willow—and *smooth, thin water-gruel* is according to Emma's father's opinion a very good thing & it is very difficult to make a cook understand what you mean by *smooth, thin water-gruel*! (Qtd in Butler 1972, p. 455)

Even Sir Walter Scott's important review praising the book in the *Quarterly Review* (see discussion in Chapter 1) included a veiled criticism along the lines of Edgeworth's: there is very little incident to the story. While praising Austen's extraordinary artistic control, Scott follows Edgeworth in lamenting what he perceived as the novel's lack of fire: "At Highbury, Cupid walks decorously, and with good discretion, bearing his torch under a lanthorn, instead of flourishing it around to set the house on fire" (Scott 1890, p. 189). The implied criticism—that the novel lacked open passion—helped frame Charlotte Brontë's famous criticisms of Austen. Of *Pride and Prejudice*, Brontë found only "a carefully fenced, highly cultivated garden, with neat borders and delicate flowers, but . . . no open country, no fresh air, no blue hill, no bonny beck" (qtd in Southam 1968, p. 126); and of *Emma* Brontë observed: "there is a Chinese fidelity, a miniature delicacy in the painting: she ruffles her reader by nothing vehement, disturbs him by nothing profound: the Passions are perfectly unknown to her . . ." (Qtd in Halperin 1975, p. 8).

Scott recorded in his journal in 1826 a revised appreciation for Austen's narrative, recognizing her purposeful avoidance of startling incidents:

> Read again, and for the third time at least, Miss Austen's very finely written novel . . . That young lady has a talent for describing the involvements and feelings and characters of ordinary life which is to me the most wonderful I ever met with. The big bow-wow strain I can do myself like any now going; but the exquisite touch, which renders ordinary commonplace things and characters interesting, from the truth of the description and the sentiment, is denied to me. (*The Journal of Sir Walter Scott*, March 14, 1826).

Here Scott's growing appreciation of Austen's unique craft prefigures the Victorians' increasing appreciation of Austen as an innovative and influential artist.

The continuing demand for Austen's work in the nineteenth century is evident in the publisher Richard Bentley's decision to republish a complete set of six novels in 1833 and in the frequency with which Austen's works are consistently cited in the diaries, memoirs, and letters of other nineteenth-century writers. And still her place as an important and major writer was uncertain in the mid-nineteenth century. The anonymous author of the 1852 review essay "Female Novelists" in the *New Monthly Magazine* observes that

Austen was not widely recognized as a major writer, and the essayist laments Austen's failure to reap "her rightful share of public homage." The challenge was answered by the prominent Victorian critic George Lewes, who observed in the *Westminster Review*, "Let Jane Austen be named, the greatest artist that has ever written" (qtd in Southam 1968, p. 244). Lewes backed up this pronouncement with the second most important review that helped establish Austen's reputation in the nineteenth-century in his prominent essay "The Novels of Jane Austen," which appeared in the highly respected serial *Blackwood's Edinburgh Magazine* in 1859.

Like Scott's initial review in 1817, Lewes's 1859 essay mixes criticism and praise and it has come down to contemporary scholars as an essential contribution to Austen studies. Brian Southam, perhaps Austen's greatest living bibliographer and historian, has described Lewes's essay as "the great appraisal." Lewes's essay is important for the way it helps articulate the qualities in Austen that drew to her works a slowly increasing Victorian audience. In "The Novels of Jane Austen," Lewes praises Austen's fiction for the more sustained pleasure the works invite in the act of re-reading. He admits to having "outlived many admirations," but the passing years have taught him only "to admire Miss Austen more." As Fiona Stafford has noted, Lewes's critical judgment as it is expressed in the essay is of a kind not open to first-time readers of a novel, but rather his assessment is based upon the opportunity and contemplation of re-reading and re-reading her works. For the essay, Lewes adopts the tone of retrospective judge, assessing which books from the earlier nineteenth century continue to draw the interest of readers—in sum, which books are enriched by multiple readings. Lewes's response to that question is deeply personal: "We never tire of her characters. They become equal to actual experiences. They live with us, and form perpetual topics of comment" (qtd in Stafford 2007, p. 9). Lewes's insight helps open an important way to exploring Austen's narrative: her narrative art is a recursive art, an art that is aware of itself and aware of the shifting sensibilities of its readers upon a second and even a third reading. This insight would prove important to the rising regard Austen would come to receive as an artist who helped guide the novel toward its own self-consciousness as an art form.

Austen's convincing representation of life, then, which Lewes considers essential to the novelist's art, results in characters sufficiently lifelike and memorable to live in the mind as real acquaintances. The execution of Austen's narrative design provides a returning reader with a recursive understanding of the foibles and unacknowledged relationships that characters hold with each other. Because of the depth of the reader's second immersion into Austen's stories, a second reading of her work proves immeasurably richer than a first. For instance, Mr. Elton's preference for Emma and not Harriet Smith becomes even more glaringly apparent on a second reading; on a second reading, the reader comes, ironically, to identify even further with Emma for mistaking Mr. Elton's design. The fact that the reader missed so many signs the first time around disposes the reader to credit Emma's mistaken perception all the more. There are many such Austen ironies that acquire a depth and volume with each new reading, and it is precisely these ironies that release to the reader the multifaceted pleasure to be found in the lifelike characterization so valued by Lewes and summed up in his observation:

> Her dramatic ventriloquism is such that, amid our tears and laughter and sympathetic exasperation at folly, we feel it almost impossible that she did not hear those very people utter those very words. In many cases this was doubtless fact. The best invention does not consist in finding *new* language for characters, but in finding the *true* language for them. (p. 100)

For Lewes, Austen's recursive narrative design and her "true language" assure that "[s]uch art as hers can never grow old, can never be superseded" (p. 112).

Like Scott, however, Lewes found Austen's art short on passion and fire. Lewes's essay ends with the reluctant admission that Austen's art lacks "power over the stormy and energetic activities which find vent in everyday life" (p. 113). Austen's lack of command over "the stormy and energetic" had been the subject of Lewes's recent correspondence with Charlotte Brontë before he completed the essay. Famously, Charlotte Brontë's criticisms of Austen appear to have influenced "the Appraisal"—and the subsequent reception of her work.

Austen had been the subject of disagreement between Lewes and Brontë since Brontë's 1859 letter asking Lewes, "Why do you like Miss Austen so very much?" After reading *Pride and Prejudice* on Lewes's recommendation, Brontë declared that she would "hardly like to live

with her ladies and gentlemen, in their elegant but confined houses,"
and she dismissed Austen's art as merely "shrewd and observant"
(*Letters* 2, 10). In keeping with Lewes's own view of Austen's fidelity
to real life, Brontë did concede: "She does her business of delineating
the surface of the lives of genteel English people curiously well; there
is . . . a miniature delicacy in the painting." But Brontë goes on to
expound upon the fault of Austen's "delineating the surface:"

> [S]he ruffles her readers by nothing vehement, disturbs him by
> nothing profound: the Passions are perfectly unknown to her;
> she rejects even a speaking acquaintance with that stormy
> Sisterhood; even to the Feelings she vouchsafes no more than an
> occasional graceful but distant recognition; too frequent con-
> verse with them would ruffle the smooth elegance of her progress.
> (Qtd in Halpein 1975, p. 8)

As Brontë continues she warms to her subject and her prose becomes
something reminiscent of Jane Eyre herself, or one of Brontë's other
fiery protagonists:

> [Austen's] business is not half so much with the human heart as
> with the human eyes, mouth, hands and feet; what sees keenly,
> speaks aptly, moves flexibly, it suits her to study, but what throbs
> fast and full, though hidden, what the blood rushes through, what
> is the unseen seat of Life and the sentient target of Death—*this*
> Miss Austen ignores. (*Letters* 2, 383)

Lewes's late admission in his otherwise celebratory assessment
and Brontë's complaint of Austen's lack of passion demonstrate a
criticism that has persisted in Austen scholarship, echoed in such
criticism as D. H. Lawrence's description of Austen as "an old maid"
whose novels lacked the "old blood-warmth" and whose works
demonstrated "the sharp knowing in apartness instead of knowing
in togetherness" (1993, pp. 303–35, esp. pp. 332–3). Further criticism along the same lines appeared in America, where American
authors were sensitive to what they perceived as the insularity of
British fiction. Ralph Waldo Emerson infamously complained in an
1861 journal entry that Austen's novels are "vulgar in tone, sterile in
artistic invention, imprisoned in the wretched conventions of
English society, without genius, wit, or knowledge of the world" (qtd

in Southam 1968, p. 28); and Twain observed that he felt "like a bar-keeper entering the kingdom of heaven" when he took up one of Austen's novels (qtd in Southam 1987, pp. 232–3).

With the assistance of Scott's celebrated review of *Emma* and Lewes's "appraisal," Austen became a popular object of rediscovery through the early and mid-Victorian period. But it was with the publication of her nephew James Edward Austen-Leigh's *A Memoir of Jane Austen* in 1870 that Austen became a publishing sensation. Austen-Leigh's loving, if thoroughly nostalgic, recounting of his aunt and her work helped make Austen a cult figure for the late Victorians. Even Austen-Leigh who held a high regard for his aunt, could not have anticipated the resurgent flood of interest that his memoir would help foster. We have to remember that during Austen's lifetime her total earnings from all of her novels came to less than £700. To put that sum in context, Maria Edgeworth, Austen's contemporary, earned almost twice that much, £11,000, for her novels which are little read today (Fergus 1997, p. 28). At the height of Austen's popularity, when she published *Emma* in 1815, Murray only printed a relatively modest 2,000 copies. Four years later in 1819, only 1,461 of those copies had sold, and the rest were remaindered. Hannah More's *Coelebs in Search of a Wife* (1808), by contrast, netted its publisher £2,000 in its first year, and went through numerous editions and 30,000 copies before More's death in 1834 (Jones 1968, p. 193). Austen's obscurity changed with Austen-Leigh's affectionate memoir that included copious extracts from Austen's letters and recounted the "Jane Austen" of subsequent legend, a quiet country rector's daughter, plying her pen as she did her needle, secure in the secluded English countryside.

The sudden boom of editions of her works brought her the popular attention she lacked in her own lifetime. Now her works achieved a popularity that placed her in the company of her first literary champion, Walter Scott, as well as the great Victorian writers Charles Dickens, Charlotte and Emily Brontë, and Anthony Trollope. But hers was a distinctive popularity: part cult, part literary celebrity. As the critic Brian Southam has chronicled, Austen's popularity in the late nineteenth century was inextricably linked to the way she was portrayed in Austen-Leigh's *Memoir*: "dear Aunt Jane" became a ladylike amateur who nonetheless possessed a genius for painting quiet pictures of a rural England that was rapidly disappearing. Austen-Leigh extolled Austen's novels almost exclusively for the care by which they delineated gentry manners, and Austen became for the late Victorians, in Southam's words, a kind of "cultural shibboleth" separating those with taste from those lacking it (1987, p. 21). In a world of increasing violence and urban vulgarity, Austen was perceived to be an antidote leading England back to its true nature. By the 1880s "Austenolatry" was in full swing. The Steventon edition of 1882 was the first collected edition of Austen works that included Austen-Leigh's *Memoir* and Austen's unpublished *Lady Susan*. The complete set of novels also included a flattering portrait of Austen and woodcut illustrations of Chawton Church and Steventon parsonage—Austen's whole world in a "tidy bundle," as Claudia Johnson observes (1997, p. 211). By the 1890s publishers were vying for the services of the leading artists of the day to assist in producing sentimentally conceived illustrations, featuring detailed period costumes, for ever newer editions of Austen's works (Duckworth 2002, p. 408).

The commercialization of Austen at the turn of the twentieth century was too much for Henry James. In "The Lesson of Balzac" (1905) he applauded the "rectification of estimate" that made Austen popular at last, but he found fault with the process by which "the body of publishers, editors, illustrators, producers of the pleasant twaddle of magazine . . . found their 'dear,' our dear, everybody's dear Jane so infinitely to their material purpose." He lamented in the popular "dear Jane": "a beguiled infatuation, a sentimentalized vision, determined largely by the accidents and circumstances originally surrounding the manifestation of genius" (qtd in Southam 1987, pp. 229–31). For all James's dislike for the popular sentiment surrounding "dear Jane" Austen, his works and his celebrated prefaces discussing the art of the novel owe much to Austen's influence. Virginia Woolf noted as much, proposing that had Austen lived longer and experienced more, she would have been "the forerunner of Henry James and of Proust." James himself intuited as much when he praised in a letter "[Austen's] narrow unconscious perfection of form" (qtd in Southam 1987, pp. 281–3). Jane Austen became a well-known, important writer as her audience widened in the nineteenth century. She began first as a writer's writer, but her popularity and importance expanded exponentially as the century drew to a close.

AUSTEN IN THE TWENTIETH CENTURY

By the twentieth century, Austen was already established as an important voice in the history of the nineteenth-century novel. Her star, however, was still rising. In 1917, on the hundredth anniversary of the author's death, Reginald Farrer published an important essay in the *Quarterly Review*. Like James, Farrer wished to separate Austen's work from the cult status that "dear Jane" had attained in the wake of her nephew's *Memoir*. Again, like James, Farrer wished to separate the genius of Austen from the image of Austen as a spinster aunt crafting small, decorous stories, or what Farrer calls the "fantasies of propriety" attaching to her reputation (p. 248), but rather in her skill in crafting her art so as to display in all of its complexity the interior life of her characters. Farrer's important study was the forerunner of Mary Lascelles's *Jane Austen and Her Art* (1939)—the first substantial academic study of Austen's novels. Lascelles' establishing text helped to usher in Austen as a major figure in literary criticism for the rest of the twentieth century.

Central to Austen's remarkable rise to eminence in the canon of English literature was her inclusion in two of the most influential books of the period: F. R. Leavis's *The Great Tradition* (1946) and Ian Watt's *The Rise of the English Novel* (1957). For Leavis, Austen inaugurates the main tradition of English fiction leading to the work of George Eliot, Henry James, and Joseph Conrad. This "Great Tradition" was characterized by technical innovation and "a marked moral intensity" (pp. 8–9). In Ian Watt's *The Rise of the Novel* (1957), Austen completes rather than initiates a fictional tradition. For Watt, Austen's achievement was to bring the novel to its mature form—especially in *Emma*—through a synthesis of Henry Fielding's objective "realism of assessment" and Samuel Richardson's subjective "realism of presentation" (pp. 296–7). Appearing at the beginning of Leavis' study and at the end of Watt's, Austen achieved a niche in the patrilineal tradition of great English authors that came to shape reading and scholarly tastes throughout the twentieth century. The fact that Austen is embraced by feminist scholars, new historicists, deconstructionalist Marxists, and virtually all cultural critics of late twentieth and early twenty-first century scholarship suggests that her central place in Western literary study is as secure as that of any English author.

As the scholar Marc DiPaolo has noted, there are two essential ways in which most scholars have read *Emma* in the twentieth and twenty-first century: (1) as a domestic Bildungsroman, and (2) as a social critique. The word Bildungsroman literally means "formation novel" and defines a storytelling mode that focuses on the maturation and education of a central protagonist. Although the genre traditionally has featured a male hero who comes of age during the course of a long, sometimes picaresque, journey, *Emma* breaks the conventions traditionally attributed to Bildungsroman by featuring a heroine who essentially stays at home. The domestic Bildungsroman school of *Emma* interpretation includes those scholars who read the novel as if it were a coming-of-age story, or a tale of moral reform. These readings, though themselves often starkly different from one another, emphasize the need for the title character to shed her snobberies, outgrow her overactive imagination, and put an end to her alienation from other women. Notably, such readings may be framed with a charitable eye towards Emma, in which case her maturation is viewed as empowering and as a normal process for a woman of her age, or they may have a more moralistic and disapproving tone, condemning Emma for her flaws and seeing the exposure of her many errors as a humorous chastening and correction of her character (DiPaolo 2007, p. 21). Prominent examples of the domestic Bildungsroman school of *Emma* include work by: Butler, Gilbert and Gubar, Kohn, Litz, Monaghan, Morgan, Mudrick, Nardin, Schorer, Tobin, and Todd (see annotations in Chapter 6: Guide to Further Reading for more about these studies).

Scholars who regard the novel as a social critique, on the other hand, view *Emma* as a story of the pressures placed on young women to conform to certain modes of behavior deemed appropriate to class, status, and gender. These interpretations generally cast Emma's home life with her hypochondriac father, Mr. Woodhouse, as a form of domestic imprisonment. Often they view her marriage to Mr. Knightley as predetermined by societal expectations, and regard the claustrophobic setting of Highbury as a site of boredom and repression. Critics who see Emma as existing in a very confining world are all the more apt to look kindly upon her revolutionary attempts to shake up the status quo with her matchmaking, her sponsorship of Harriet, and her reluctance to marry and befriend those whom society demand that she marry and befriend (DiPaolo 2007, p. 22). Important examples of the social critique school of *Emma* include: Finch and Bowen, Johnson, Mukherjee, and Sulloway (see Chapter 6: Guide to Further Reading for more about these studies).

PUBLISHING HISTORY

Emma was published late in 1815 (December 23), though the date on the title page is 1816. The publisher, John Murray, ordered a press run of 2,000 copies with the retail price for the three volumes set at 21 shillings. By October 1816 a little over half of the copies had been sold (1,200), and they earned for Jane Austen a profit of some £221.

No manuscript of *Emma* survives, and no other edition appeared in Jane Austen's lifetime. The three-volume first edition consequently holds special authority. It was not until 1833 that *Emma* was reprinted, when Richard Bentley produced a collected edition of Austen's novels as part of his series of Standard English Novels. Bentley's print runs were modest, around 2,500. The sales of Bentley's Standard English Novel edition of *Emma* were not swift. It was only in 1836 that a new impression was called for. There were further impression and print runs of this edition in 1836, 1841, and 1860. By the 1860s, *Emma* was out of copyright and other publishers such as Simms, M'Intyre, and Routledge were bringing out editions of the novel. In 1870, as we have noted, Austen's work became enormously popular in response to the publication of Austen-Leigh's *Memoir of Jane Austen*. Since 1880 *Emma* has been continuously in print, and for almost all of that time there has been a choice between several editions. The first edition of the novel that makes editorial claims to primacy is the set of the novels in ten volumes edited by Reginald Brimley Johnson for Dent. Although the Dent edition is important, the authoritative and establishing text of Jane Austen's novels owes everything to R. W. Chapman's emendations for the edition of Austen's works he produced for Oxford University Press in 1923. All subsequent editions of *Emma* have attended to Chapman, although David Gilson's 2002 survey of the Jane Austen texts suggests that we should not continue to be overly deferential to the texts Chapman has established.

STUDY QUESTIONS FOR CHAPTER 4

1. Critics such as Walter Scott, Charlotte Brontë, and D. H. Lawrence have complained that Austen's novels, including *Emma*, lack passion. Memorably, Mark Twain observed that he felt "like a barkeeper entering the kingdom of heaven" when he took up one of Austen's novels. Do you agree with such criticism? If so, why, and if not, why not?

2. The two most common ways of reading Austen's *Emma* are as a domestic Bildungsroman, or as a social critique. Describe these two types of approaches: what are their interests, concerns, and approaches? Does your interpretation of the novel fall into either camp?

3. Jane Austen has always been considered a writer's writer, long before she became a canonical and widely taught author. What specific qualities draw the appreciation of so many other authors?

4. This chapter has traced Austen's rise to prominence as a major author in the English literary tradition. To what four or five books is Austen's high reputation most indebted?

CHAPTER 5

ADAPTATION, INTERPRETATION, AND INFLUENCE

Jane Austen's *Emma*, like all of Austen's novels, has been richly embraced by the media of television and film. The first filmed adaptation of *Emma* appeared in 1948 as a 105-minute live television production written and produced by Judy Campbell and aired on the BBC. Campbell's adaptation of *Emma* was the first of five adaptations made for British and American television between the 1940s and the 1970s. The first American-based television adaptation of the novel was the hour-long live production broadcast on November 24, 1954 of *Emma* as an episode of NBC Kraft Television Theater. The other television adaptations include: Vincent Tilsley's *"Emma"* (1960), and the Glenister-Constanduros version (1972). More familiar to students will the three film adaptations that appeared in the 1990s: *Clueless* (1995), a popular-culture adaptation, written and directed by Amy Heckerling and starring Alicia Silverstone; *Emma* (1996), an American film written and directed by Douglas McGrath and starring Gwyneth Paltrow; and *Jane Austen's "Emma"* (1996), a British television production written by Andrew Davies, directed by Diarmuid Lawrence, and starring Kate Beckinsale. We shall focus on each of the television and film adaptations in date order, except for the loosely adapted film *Clueless*, which we will consider last.

THE FIRST TELEVISION PRODUCTION (1948)
"EMMA." MAY 24, 1948. (BBC, LIVE, B&W, 105 MINUTES)

The first *Emma* was an adaptation written and produced by Judy Campbell and performed for live television broadcast on BBC TV on Sunday May 23, 1948. Campbell's adaptation cleverly focuses on the place of gossip in Austen's novel. By dramatizing gossip as action, Campbell points the way to future film adaptation replicating Austen's narrative technique of free indirect discourse (see Chapter 2: Language and Style). Campbell's screenplay replicates the charm of Austen's Highbury as well as the rigid class structure depicted in the novel. Campbell's *"Emma"* centers the novels action among the gossipy conversations that unfold in Ford's shop (a relatively minor local in Austen's text). Most significant to this *Emma* are scenes in which Miss Bates and Mrs. Ford exchange rumors as they conduct the important community business of gossip, serving as a source of news, as a means of knitting together the community, and as a manner of influencing the behavior of their Highbury neighbors.

Because of the live production's comparatively brief running time and the studio-bound nature of its performance, the production demanded that the action of the novel be compressed through significant cuts and alterations to Austen's tale. Significantly, the changes to the story structure that Campbell made would later become standard alterations for most of the adaptations that would follow. For instance, in Campbell's *"Emma,"* as in the majority of the other film and television depictions, the Box Hill excursion and the strawberry picking at Donwell Abbey are dramatized as taking place in a single afternoon. The most notable feature is the magnified role Mr. Perry plays and the focus on gossip at Ford's, presented in Campbell's version, as the domain of the most gossipy character in Highbury, Miss Bates.

As Marc DiPaolo (2007) has noted, the special attention that Campbell pays to Miss Bates and the Jane Fairfax plot, shifts the focus of the story away from Emma, and offers a more distant, mediated view of Emma's gradual transformation than the novel does. Part of Campbell's special attention to the Bateses and Jane Fairfax appears deliberate, since Campbell's *"Emma"* is more interested in portraying the financial and emotional crisis that Jane is enduring, and is less interested in Emma's confining situation. The consequence of Campbell's interpretation and performance of Austen's text is that Campbell's version of *Emma* reads the novel as a social critique instead of as a domestic Bildungsroman (ibid., pp. 44–5) (see Chapter 4 of this book for details regarding this distinction).

THE SECOND TELEVISION PRODUCTION (1954)
"EMMA." NOVEMBER 24, 1954. (NBC, B&W, 60 MINUTES)

The first American-based television adaptation of the novel is memorable simply because it is so bad. An hour-long live broadcast produced as an episode of *NBC Kraft Television Theater*, this *"Emma"* stars Felicia Montealegre as Emma and Peter Cookson as Mr. Knightley. The production omits virtually all of the supporting characters, including Miss and Mrs. Bates, Robert Martin, Frank Churchill, Jane Fairfax, and Isabella and John Knightley. The production attempts to play Austen's novel up for light laughs. It transposes the relatively minor character William Larkins, Mr. Knightley's overseer, into the role played by Robert Martin in Austen's text.

In the place of the more serious elements of Austen's novel including the Jane Fairfax and Frank Churchill subplot, the Kraft adaptation presents a series of originally conceived comic interludes that contribute to its tone of broad humor and farce. For instance, William Larkins (the substitute Robert Martin figure) plays up the role of the country bumpkin by waxing poetic about the birth of a litter of pigs: "We got the finest litter of pigs you ever saw . . . from Polly, your pig, Harriet. Oh, bless her old sow's heart!" Similarly, Harriet rushes into Hartfield, frantic that "Old Jim" the bull has gotten free and that William has had a terrible time catching him, drawing from Mr. Knightley the following observation: "If I can't rescue Emma from herself, I can rescue William from a bull." The focus of the production little resembles the Austen plot, but rather rests on the love triangle between Harriet, Mr. Elton, and William Larkins. Students who pursue obtaining a copy and watching the production may be reminded of the irreverent, slapstick comedy of the television cartoon *South Park* on The Comedy Channel.

The most valuable insight to be gleaned from this production is what this adaptation says, not about Austen's *Emma*, but about American popular comic taste in the 1950s. William Larkins as a country bumpkin serves up the incongruous low comedy that is typical of American television of the period. The emphasis on Larkins' cultural and intellectual inferiority, rather than class difference serves to elide class as a social marker for American audiences. Similarly, for Harriet, there is no reference of her being of low origins; rather her inferiority resides in her silliness and her lack of polished manners. Austen's serious map of class difference and its powerful effect on social interaction is blissfully ignored, with the comic fiction that character traits, not class difference, determine the American social order.

THE THIRD TELEVISION PRODUCTION (1960)
"EMMA." FEBRUARY 26—APRIL 6, 1960. (BBC, B&W, 180 MINUTES)

One of the longest form adaptations of Austen's novel for television is Vincent Tilsley's 1960 screenplay and adaptation. This six-part production with a total running time of 180 minutes, a live BBC miniseries broadcast, helped facilitate later more complete renderings of Austen's novel to film. One of the most remarkable features of Tilsley's "*Emma*," however, is its willingness to create new scenes that decidedly cast Highbury's ruling class in an unsympathetic light. These new scenes, entirely original to Tilsley, focus on the darker side of Emma and Mr. Knightley, as well as on the villainy of Mrs. Churchill and Mrs. Elton. The effect is to show the privileged characters in Austen's story—Emma, Mr. Knightley, Mr. Woodhouse, and Mrs. Elton—neglecting or actively tormenting the members of the Highbury community who depend upon them for support. Such new scenes tend to throw into a much more positive light the characters in dependent circumstances: Jane Fairfax, Harriet Smith, Robert Martin, and Miss Bates. Even Mr. Weston and Frank Churchill are improved by Tilsley's additions, now portrayed as victims of a failed patronage system. Tilsley's thematic emphasis on issues of class-based competition and jealousies push this adaptation into portraying Austen's novel as a social critique rather than as a domestic Bildungsroman.

THE FOURTH TELEVISION PRODUCTION (1972)
"EMMA." 1972. (BBC2, COLOR, 5-PARTS, 257 MINUTES)

Written by Denis Constanduros and directed by John Glenister, the fourth television production of *Emma* was a miniseries first broadcast on BBC2 in 1972. This miniseries (commonly referred to by critics as the "Glenister-Constanduros version") is the longest of all *Emma* adaptations and scrupulously faithful to Austen's novel. Essentially, all of the key scenes in the development of the plot are transcribed to film. Even elements of the novel every other adaptation excises find its way into this production. For instance, the Glenister-Constanduros *Emma* is the only adaptation to include Mrs. Weston's pregnancy and to feature John and Isabella Knightley in anything beyond a cameo appearance. Constanduros strove to, as he notes, "preserve as much as possible the flavour of Jane Austen's language" (Lauritzen 1981, p. 127).

One of the central reasons the Glenister-Constanduros version is so interesting to modern audiences, aside from the thoroughness of its adaptation, is the production's passionless portrayal of Emma's attraction to Mr. Knightley. The series casts John Carson as Mr. Knightley, described by the critic Sue Parrill as "paunchy and graying" and one who "exudes solidity and complacency" as he "emphasizes the age difference between Emma and Mr. Knightley" (p. 124). The connection between Emma and Mr. Knightley in the production draws out the tutor and mentor relationship of Austen's story. Unique for the mediums of film and television, the ending does not feature a climatic kiss accompanied by a swell in the music score.

The earnest quality of this production's adherence to Austen's novel proves to be not only its greatest strength, but also its greatest weakness. Austen scholars often criticize this production for being too bland and conservative in its staging and too staid in dramatizing Emma's emotional and intellectual life. Even though Emma does grow and change as a character during the course of the Glenister-Constanduros version, the adaptation does not succeed as a domestic Bildungsroman production because of its failure to emphasize the workings of Emma's mind appropriately. Portraying Austen's story as a social critique is more successful in this version. The stage-bound, claustrophobic atmosphere of the miniseries reinforces the lack of control Emma has over her environment. The simple sets seem to close in on Emma in key scenes, especially when she is shown gazing out the window at the outside world that the sickly Mr. Woodhouse has denied her. As Marc DiPalo has noted, this, indeed, is an Emma that is "seldom ever two hours from Hartfield" (*Emma*, p. 252), and who complains to Mr. John Knightley that attending two dinner parties and making plans for a ball that is cancelled hardly constitutes an abundance of "visiting-engagements" (*Emma*, p. 251; DiPaolo 2007, p. 76).

THE FIRST FILM PRODUCTION (1996)
EMMA. RELEASED AUGUST 2 (US), SEPTEMBER 13, 1996 (UK).
(COLUMBIA/MIRAMAX MOTION PICTURE, COLOR, 120 MINUTES)

The 1996 Douglas McGrath adaptation differs from those that came before by portraying the marriage of Emma and Mr. Knightley as the ultimate union of equals. The focus of the film is sharply limited to the romance of Emma and Mr. Knightley, taking up Austen's novel as a domestic Bildungsroman and portraying Emma's story not as a form of moral parable, inviting the audience to judge Emma's faults, but rather as a coming-of-age story affirming and celebrating Emma's natural goodness. Gone are some of the darker hues to Emma's character. Gwyneth Paltrow's sympathetic and lively portrayal of Emma distances itself from the unpleasant qualities of Austen's original, about whom Austen predicted, "no one but myself will much like." Although the film chastises Emma strongly for insulting Miss Bates at Box Hill, and celebrates her eventual penance for such snobbishness, the film evokes enough sympathy for Emma by depicting her inner life through voiceovers and telling close-ups of the visually stunning Paltrow, to such effect that Emma emerges as more likeable and more the heroine of Austen's tale than she does in any of the earlier, or later, adaptations.

In addition to granting Emma more subjectivity than the preceding television versions did, the McGrath film is unique in the physical emphasis on Emma's health and vitality. In this way, the McGrath film stands alone in drawing out a subject of much interest to contemporary scholars, "Nervousness and Health" (see also Chapter 6). Two of McGrath's wholly original scenes draw out Emma's appealing vitality and strength. McGrath's Emma counts archery as one of her hobbies and she drives herself from place to place in a carriage without the assistance of James to accompany her. Such physicality holds a powerful place in the visual re-telling of Austen's story. Emma's archery captures her daring and reflects the emerging feminism that has made Austen a contemporary favorite in feminist studies. The critic Suzanne Ferriss finds these liberties with the text to be successful aspects of McGrath's production:

> Archery, for instance, was a newly popular sport among the upper classes, with women competing directly against men . . . The image of Emma engaging simultaneously in athletic and verbal

competition with Knightley has particular resonance for contemporary women, who are exhorted regularly to 'just do it' like their male counterparts. McGrath's version thus offers an active, competitive heroine, whose physical daring mirrors her outspokenness and verbal self-confidence. In the film, Emma accuses men of 'preferring superficial qualities' such as physical beauty, a charge that clearly invokes contemporary feminist objections to the over-emphasis on the female body characteristic of consumer culture. (p. 127)

Such liberating physicality, however, is subsumed, most critics would say, by the film's ultimately paternalistic impulse. Emma's moral inferiority to Knightley is reflected by her inferior skill as an archer, and when Emma proves too headstrong and lodges her carriage into a large pool of water, Frank Churchill comes to the rescue on horseback.

Like Emma, the character of Mr. Knightley is blanched of some of his darker hues and refigured to be more sympathetic in McGrath's film. Played by the handsome Jeremy Northam, Mr. Knightley in the Miramax film is a smaller man than the Mr. Knightleys of earlier adaptations. Northam is uniquely successful in drawing out the good humor and sensitivity in Austen's Mr. Knightley—and this goes a long way toward strengthening the romantic focus of McGrath's film. Northam's acting style is understated and he is good at portraying Austen's sly irony. For instance, in the scene in which he and Emma compete at shooting arrows at a target, when Emma's loses focus and misses the target entirely, he quips, "Please don't kill my dogs." In another scene, in which he is standing with the massive and imposing Donwell Abbey behind him, he tells Emma he would rather not go to the ball but would prefer to stay at home, "Where it's cozy." Such self-deprecating humor, though present in Austen's Mr. Knightley, warms even further the appeal of Northam's Knightley.

Just as McGrath's film highlights the penance Emma feels for insulting Miss Bates, the film also highlights Mr. Knightley's need to relax his stodginess and stiffness of manner. For instance, in McGrath's reworking of the scene in which Mrs. Weston and Emma interrogate Mr. Knightley about his feelings for Jane Fairfax, Northam's Knightley is so uncomfortable with the suggestion of his desiring Miss Fairfax that he flees the conversation. The flashes of self-deprecating humor that Paltrow's Emma helps elicit from

Northam's Knightley serve to thaw and warm Mr. Knightley as a romantic object. As two flawed-but-sympathetic characters, Northam's Knightley and Paltrow's Emma mature and grow during the course of the film and prove themselves worthy of one another's love by acknowledging shortcomings in themselves and in each other. By working to amend and accept their flaws, McGrath makes clear his film's reading of Austen's *Emma* as a domestic Bildungsroman. The moral of McGrath's reading is tidily summed up during the proposal scene, when McGrath strays from Austen's text and has Mr. Knightley say, "Perhaps it is our imperfections that make us so perfect for one another."

THE SECOND FILM PRODUCTION (1996)
JANE AUSTEN'S "EMMA". 1996 (UK) FEBRUARY 16, 1997 (US).
(MERIDIAN-ITV/A&E "TELEMOVIE," COLOR, 107 MINUTES)

Director Diarmuid Lawrence and screenwriter Andrew Davies produced what is probably the best of the television and film adaptations of *Emma* with their highly innovative and engaging *Jane Austen's "Emma"*. Starring Kate Beckinsale as Emma, this Meridian-ITV/A&E television movie draws on radical and progressive critical literary readings, as well as screenwriter Andrew Davies's thorough knowledge of Austen scholarship. By dramatizing psychoanalytic theory and Marxist-historical interpretations, the Lawrence–Davis *Emma* attempts to practice in film some of the innovative narrative techniques Austen's *Emma* helped to pioneer in fiction. The production additionally evaluates and criticizes aspects of the Regency period it depicts, especially the rigid class structure, while praising the powerful, wealthy Mr. Knightley for demonstrating a greater sense of civic responsibility and justice than contemporary globalist corporations—the capitalist equivalent of Mr. Knightley in the book with regard to wealth.

While McGrath's *Emma* embraces a reading of the novel that focuses on the successful romance between Emma and Mr. Knightley as the natural outcome of the film's domestic Bildungsroman focus, the Lawrence–Davies film accentuates darker aspects of the Emma–Knightley relationship, shadowing the original text. In the Lawrence–Davies film, Mr. Knightley is clearly the more dominant personality, and he retains more of the morally righteous attitude softened by McGrath. Lawrence–Davies's Knightley has far more of a temper than McGrath's and his general bearing is far more imposing. Consequently, the relationship between Emma and Mr. Knightley is not the sunny attraction of equals depicted in McGrath, but rather a more complex and darker attraction related to the complex psychological needs and drives depicted in Austen's *Emma*.

The Lawrence–Davies *Jane Austen's "Emma"* makes use of recent psychoanalytic readings of the Emma–Knightley relationship, especially Frances L. Restuccia's celebrated 1994 essay "A Black Morning: Kristevan Melancholia in Jane Austen's *Emma*." Since Emma's love object, Mr. Knightley, is old enough to be her father and is fond of referring to her as "a spoiled child" or as "little Emma," both Restuccia and Lawrence–Davies interpret the attraction between Emma and Knightley as Freudian in nature, a complex response to Emma's loss of Mrs. Woodhouse in childhood and her loss to marriage of her surrogate mother, Mrs. Weston, at the beginning of the book. Both the Lawrence–Davies *Jane Austen's "Emma"* and Austen's *Emma* accentuate the double maternal loss that initiates the story's action. Accordingly, Emma's matchmaking enterprises prove an outlet for her psychic quest for her absent mother: by vicariously pursuing the attachments of others, Emma can express her own longing, while distancing herself from the potential *re-wounding* loss of herself becoming attached. As Restuccia observes, and the Lawrence–Davies adaptation helps perform: "Emma begins by offering a glimpse into the abyss—sustained throughout the novel by the accumulation of lost, dead, and dying mothers—for which [Emma's quest in the novel] attempts to provide compensation" (p. 453). The loss of Miss Taylor echoes across the tale, as the loss of Emma's mother is expressed in Emma's repressed desire to marry Mr. Knightley—the parental figure who is least likely to abandon her. Only the potential loss of Mr. Knightley to Harriet Smith at the end of the novel allows Emma's desire to become realized and expressed. The rich qualities of this psychodrama, subtly played out in Austen's text, are ignored in most television and film adaptations. But the Lawrence–Davies *Jane Austen's "Emma"* successfully explores and portrays the sophisticated romance between Emma and Mr. Knightley. Gone is the Hollywood glamour of McGrath's pleasing, if uncomplicated, romance. But it is replaced instead with something much more in keeping with the psychological complexity of Austen's original

The Lawrence–Davies film is right not to follow too far in darkly psychoanalyzing Austen's text. According to Restuccia's reading, the marriage to Mr. Knightley is portended to be a mistake by Austen. She writes:

> It might be tempting to ignore Knightley's linkage with Emma's mother and to conceive of the marriage at the end of the novel as a triumph in which all traces of the mother are wiped out, her loss negated, but such a reading is undercut by Emma's altered behavior on becoming engaged to Mr Knightley. In the last chapters, we find Emma parroting Mr Knightley's views (especially on Harriet) and failing to speak, as if in rehearsal for what promises to be a silencing marriage celebrated at the very end. The Emma we knew, sparkling with wit, is reduced to insipid remarks of gratitude to Knightley. (pp. 460–8; qtd in DiPaolo 2007, p. 107)

For Restuccia, Emma's unresolved feelings of grief over her mother's premature death cause her to seek out a parental replacement, Mr. Knightley, as an inappropriate and almost incestuous love match, forever preventing her from recovering from her mother's death. Restuccia's cynical dismissal of the possibility of love, even a love as complex and psychically driven as Emma's love for Mr. Knightley, overplays its hand. For all of its subtle incorporation of Restuccia's celebrated interpretation, the film is right to stop short of reducing the novel to a portrait of mental illness. The Lawrence–Davies adaptation, while acknowledging the psychological drives and needs motivating Emma's attraction to Mr. Knightley, still sides with the original's romantic, Bildungsroman strain: Emma and Mr. Knightley mature through their interactions ultimately finding moral and spiritual growth in their union.

Perhaps even more innovative than Lawrence–Davies's psychoanalytical depiction of *Emma* is the work's bold willingness to try to match the novel's narrative innovations by reproducing them with innovative film techniques. Chief among these is the attempt to bring to film Austen's technique of free indirect discourse by making manifest Emma's thought-processes as well as an overarching perspective related to Austen's third-person narrator (see Chapter 2). At the same time that the film works to present an unfiltered view of Emma's perceptions of reality by depicting her imaginative journeys as filmic flash-forwards (instead of flashbacks), the film also explores the incongruity of splitting the perspective between Emma herself and the servants by matching Emma's mental journey with a type of omniscient third person. The emphasis on the servants' perspective is wholly original to this production, but it does help expand the associative perspective of the camera beyond simply Emma. In this way, the original focus on servants that have no identity in Austen's text become third-person witnesses to the original *Emma*. Like Austen's free indirect discourse, which presents "dual voices," the voices of the narrator and Emma at once (see again Chapter 2), Lawrence–Davies manage to tell the story through two radically different narrative lenses simultaneously—presenting Emma's own fanciful outlook on events that contrast sharply with the perspective also depicted by the perspective of the less financially and socially powerful members of Highbury.

Ultimately, it is the Lawrence—Davies device of practicing free indirect discourse both narratively and visually that determines the emphasis of their *Emma*. While their film does successfully portray the domestic Bildungsroman of Emma's moral growth culminating in her marriage to Mr. Knightley, the film's focus and emphasis sides with *Emma* as a social critique. In the Lawrence–Davies film, Emma's chief fault is that her imagination clouds her perceptions of reality to the point that she is blind to the very real suffering of Harriet, who would be happier marrying Robert Martin than Emma is willing to admit. So, too, is Emma too caught up in her imaginary perceptions to see that Jane Fairfax's love life is far less romantic and far more troubled than she can understand. The refreshing perspective of life from the servants prospective further underscores Emma's unfeeling blindness. They go to great lengths setting up the heavy furniture and the other social accoutrements of the Box Hill party, only so that an awkward and upsetting afternoon can be experienced by Highbury's gentry class outdoors. In this fashion, the Lawrence–Davies film portrays Emma as a misguided figure with a snobbish streak and a very vivid imagination that needs to observe (as we the audience do) with great clarity and empathy the people who populate the community of Highbury.

THE THIRD FILM PRODUCTION (1995)
CLUELESS. RELEASED JULY 19, (US) OCTOBER 20, 1995 (US).
(PARAMOUNT MOTION PICTURE, COLOR, 113 MINUTES)

Clueless constitutes an instance where the sophisticated literary criticism that the movie has garnered is far more interesting than the work itself. Time spent watching the film would be better spent reading the interesting interpretations of the film's critics. As an object of popular culture, created and marketed as a "teen film" from a major film studio, the focus of the movie is not on adapting Austen's *Emma* to the medium of film. Rather, *Clueless* is an analogy adaptation in which the movie's structure and plot are based on Austen's *Emma*. Writer-director Amy Heckerling lifts Austen's story out of the Regency period and places it in present-day California at the time of its filming (1995). The result is a shallow, big budget film that nonetheless becomes endlessly interesting when joined to Austen's classic novel.

Remembering that she loved reading *Emma* in college, Heckerling decided that Austen's novel was the ideal book to choose as a template for *Clueless* because "[t]he plot is perfect for any time" (*Rolling Stone*. August 22, 1996). In writing *Clueless*, Heckerling drew upon Austen's "sense of class and social dynamic" for inspiration and used *Emma* as a "structural tree." Heckerling describes how she was inspired to make the 1995 film:

> I wanted to do a happy movie about a very optimistic young girl . . . I really had her attitude in my head, and what I thought I needed was a strong structure in the style of comedy of manners. (Qtd in DiPaolo 2007, p. 125).

Heckerling is successful in creating what she sets out to do: provide "a happy movie about a very optimistic young girl." Though Heckerling's heroine lacks much of the sophistication of Austen's *Emma*, the heroine of Heckerling's film, Cher, has drawn a great deal of scholarly interest. For scholars who see *Clueless* as a purposeful adaptation of *Emma*, the film finds fascinating contemporary parallels for Austen's ironic narrative tone. For these observers, *Clueless* echoes Austen's concern with the shifting social mores of a turbulent socio-political era, and recreates the novel's ambivalent depiction of provincial life. Heckerling recasts the 21-year-old Emma Woodhouse as American high school student Cher Horowitz, and turns most members of the novel's supporting cast into Cher's classmates, providing them California-style names based on American celebrities, while also introducing characters with racially and ethnically diverse backgrounds. The success of the film's attempt to portray a late twentieth-century "multiculturalism," however, is dubious, as the scholarship on the film makes clear. The film's Mr. Knightley figure is an undergraduate philosophy major named Josh.

At the start of the film, Cher seems to demonstrate great potential that she is not managing to reach because she, as her father puts it, lacks "direction." She possesses a rich vocabulary (relative to the valley-speak of most of her peers) and is capable of negotiating better grades from her teachers. She demonstrates knowledge of fashion, and like Emma Woodhouse, she styles herself as a matchmaker. Significantly, Cher is markedly less intelligent than the character that inspired her creation, and in part, due to her age (16), Cher has a much longer road to travel to reach maturity than Austen's Emma has. The film strains to depict Cher's moral growth by demonstrating an increased knowledge of literature and an improved grasp of international policy and global poverty—though the film's portrayal of both still betray shallowness and immaturity. Other themes for Cher in Heckerling's film include a more thorough understanding of romantic relationships and a more sophisticated understanding of sexuality. By the end of the film, Heckerling attempts to show Cher developing intellectually, emotionally, and morally, clearly adapting *Clueless* to Austen's theme of the Bildungsroman.

The best and most thorough literary analysis of *Clueless* is Gayle Wald's postcolonial treatment, "*Clueless* in the Neo-Colonial World Order" (2000). Once the reader gets over the astonishment that anyone would apply Wald's theoretical pyrotechnics to *Clueless*, her postcolonial treatment proves an exciting cultural studies approach to the subject of the commodification of literary adaptation—intellectually, the most promising and fruitful path of study in relation to Heckerling's film. For Wald, the "Americanization" of *Emma* makes Austen's wealthy heroine "the unwitting heiress of British imperial and colonial enterprises." Wald's far-reaching response to the film's reception and commodification emphasizes power relations, citizenship, consumerism, private experience, and gendered agency. The essay invites skeptics to take the film—or at least the cultural criticism treating it—seriously.

It is fitting that in releasing *Clueless*, Paramount Studios steered clear of relating the film to Austen's novel for fear that any perceived literary quality would turn away teenagers. The fact that the film was a blockbuster hit is telling, because its original audiences found much comfort in the film's formulaic representation of its teen subjects.

And yet, precisely because it is an object of popular culture, and because it has developed an amazingly sophisticated scholarship, *Clueless* is an essential part of the history of *Emma*'s adaptation.

STUDY QUESTIONS FOR CHAPTER 5

1. Of the various *Emma* adaptations, which do you find the most interesting and why? Are there any ways in which the adaptation you favor improves upon Austen's original text?

2. If you were to adapt Austen's *Emma* for a contemporary "teen-flick" and you had the backing of a major studio such as Paramount, how would you update *Emma* for a contemporary teen audience? Remember, the film company is investing in a big-budget enterprise, and they need to fill seats! What scenes and characters would you include from Austen, and how might you update these to appeal to the teenage demographic? What actors and actresses might you cast for different characters? What, if anything, might you add to your script?

3. Review the literary technique of free indirect discourse (see Chapter 2). Now consider how this technique is handled in one of the television of film adaptations. How do you present such a literary technique best in the visual medium of television and film?

4. With a group of friends, or with fellow students, choose one scene from Austen's *Emma* to adapt. Now plan the costumes, dialogue, and camera angles of your production. Proceed to film your production digitally. Did your intended interpretation of the scene materialize in your filmic adaptation?

5. View the 1996 Gwyneth Paltrow/Miramax version of *Emma*. Now view one of the other adaptations noted in this chapter. Write a paper comparing these two film interpretation to Austen's novel. What themes and devices from Austen's fiction do both productions maintain? What is lost? Which is the better adaptation? And why?

Be sure to consider Dudley Andrews definition of "adaptation" in the book *Film and Literature*: pp. 262–72.
Useful research might include:

- Corrigan, Timothy, *Film and Literature: An Introduction and Reader*. (Chapters 5, 6, and 7); George Bluestone's "The Limits

of the Novel and the Limits of the Film"; and Dudley Andrew's "Adaptation"): pp. 55–88; 197– 212; and 262–72.
- Parrill, Sue, *Jane Austen on Film and Television* (Jefferson, NC and London: McFarland and Company 2002) (Chapter 1—"Why Jane Austen?": pp. 3–15; and Chapter 5—"Emma": pp. 7–47)

CHAPTER 6

GUIDE TO FURTHER READING

POETRY

Jane Austen: Collected Poems and Verse of the Austen Family, ed. David Selwyn. Manchester: Carcanet Press, 1996.

LETTERS

Jane Austen's Letters, 3rd edition, ed. Deirdre Le Faye (Oxford: Oxford University Press, 1995).

Jane Austen's Letters to Her Sister Cassandra and Others, ed. R. W. Chapman (London and New York, 1932; rev. ed., 1952; repr. 1959). A selection is available in the Oxford World Classics series: *Jane Austen's Letters 1796–1817*, ed. R. W. Chapman. Oxford: Oxford University Press 1955; repr. 1956, 1966.

Jane Austen's Literary Manuscripts: A Study of the Novelist's Development Through the Surviving Papers, ed. Brian Southam, 2nd rev. ed. (New York and London: Continuum, 2002).

BIOGRAPHIES

The field of Austen biography is a crowded and competitive one. With relatively little source material, the difference in the many biographies is in inflection and focus. Fortunately, many of the best male and female practitioners of the biography have written accounts of Jane Austen's life.

Austen, Caroline, *My Aunt Jane: A Memoir* (Alton: The Jane Austen Society, 1952).

Austen-Leigh, James, *A Memoir of Jane Austen*, 1870, ed. Kathryn Sutherland (Oxford: Oxford University Press, 2002). This is the memoir that helped to popularize Jane in the late Victorian period. While launching Austen's sudden rise into canonical literature, this memoir also helped to construct the nostalgic "dear Jane" figure from which the real Jane Austen is still trying to emerge.

Halperin, John, *The Life of Jane Austen* (Baltimore: Johns Hopkins University Press, 1984). One of the most readable and straightforward of the Austen biographies, notable for its refusal to romanticize Austen's life. Students of *Emma* will find a very fine general discussion here.

Honan, Park, *Jane Austen: Her Life* (New York: St. Martin's Press, 1987). Honan's still important *Life* is unique in the detailed attention to Austen's relationships with her brothers, and the way these relationships brought Austen more squarely into the social, political, and economic upheavals of her day. Honan's biography is strong on social history, if a little weak in its depiction of Austen and her psychology.

Jenkins, Elizabeth, *Jane Austen* (New York: Pellegrini and Cudahy, 1949). Perhaps the most thorough and detailed account of Austen's life. For the student serious about uncovering the fine-grain details of Austen's life, this is the place to turn.

Nokes, David, *Jane Austen: A Life* (Berkeley and Los Angeles: University of California Press, 1997). Nokes' biography draws most heavily on Austen's letters. The account of Austen here is fascinating for its unique emphasis on a "rebellious, satirical, and wild" Austen. Nokes takes as his starting point Austen's observation, "If I am a wild beast, I cannot help it. It is not my own fault." If at times, the biography appears to overcompensate in emphasizing Austen's unruliness, but the effort is useful as a corrective to the long ossified view of "dear Jane."

Shields, Carol, *Jane Austen (Penguin Lives)* (New York: Viking, 2001). This slim account of Austen by an award-winning Canadian novelist is probably the best place to start for a student coming to Austen's life for the first time. Shields' economy, wit, and incisive selection of materials to emphasize make it the single most entertaining life of Austen.

Tomalin, Claire, *Jane Austen: A Life* (New York: Alfred A. Knopf, 1997). The strength of Tomalin's biography is its attention to, and compassion regarding, the child-rearing practices of the Austens and the physical demands on child-bearing women, elements usually overlooked by Austen's many male biographers.

BIBLIOGRAPHY

Chapman, R. W., *Jane Austen: A Critical Bibliography* (Oxford: Clarendon Press, 1953).

Gibson, David, *A Bibliography of Jane Austen* (Oxford: Clarendon Press, 1982).

Roth, Barry, *An Annotated Bibliography of Jane Austen Studies, 1984–1994* (Athens: Ohio University Press, 1996).

Roth, Barry, *An Annotated Bibliography of Jane Austen Studies, 1973–1983* (Charlottesville: University Press of Virginia, 1985).

Roth, Barry, and Joel Weinsheimer, *An Annotated Bibliography of Jane Austen Studies, 1952–1972* (Charlottesville: University Press of Virginia, 1973).

Stafford, Fiona, "Jane Austen," in *Literature of the Romantic Period: A Bibliographical Guide*, ed. Michael O'Neill (Oxford: Oxford University Press, 1998: pp. 246–68).

CRITICISM

This section is subdivided to match the chapters and sections in the guide. Where critical books or essays have been cited in my study, the bibliographical details are provided below, along with a brief annotation. Where a critical book or essay is included here for the first time, annotation assessing its value and identifying its main topic(s) is supplied.

Contexts

Auden, W. H., "Letter to Lord Byron" in *Letters from Iceland* (New York: Random House, 1937).

Butler, Marilyn, *Jane Austen and the War of Ideas* (Oxford: Clarendon Press, 1975). Butler's method of investigation is to survey the political allegiances of other novels of the period, thus establishing a convincing intellectual context for Austen's work. The moral issues in Austen's text are accordingly read as reflections of eighteenth-century philosophical enquiries into human nature, which had turned deeply political in their implications for readers during the French Revolution. The opposition between reason and passion, self-interest and selflessness, and individual ambition and social responsibility were endlessly explored in the fiction of the 1790s. By placing Austen's work within this context, Butler finds in Austen a devoted conservative; her literary manner is defined as "that of a conservative Christian moralist of the 1790s."

Duckworth, Alistair, *The Improvement of the Estate* (Baltimore: Johns Hopkins University Press, 1971). Duckworth, like most critics of the 1970s and early 1980s, emphasizes Austen's moral seriousness. He does so by pointing out strong connections between Austen's novels and the writings of Edmund Burke. He writes: "Jane Austen affirms society, ideally considered as a structure of values that are ultimately founded in religious principle, at the same time as she distinguishes it from its frequently corrupted form." Typically, her plots chart the individual's course from an initial inherited security through an intermediate estrangement and finally to a reintegration with society. Like Marilyn Butler's *Jane Austen and the War of Ideas*, Duckworth's *The Improvement of the Estate* is one of the most formidable arguments for Austen as a political and social conservative.

Scott, Walter, "Review of *Emma*," *Quarterly Review* 14 (October, 1815 [March 1816]), pp. 188–201.

Thelwall, John, *The Peripatetic*, ed. Judith Thompson (Detroit: Wayne State University Press, 2001). Thelwall was a radical British orator and writer. Judith Thompson's new scholarly edition of Thelwall's important sketches provide wonderful source material for investigating the social and political context of the Romantic period.

Todd, Janet, *The Cambridge Guide to Jane Austen* (Cambridge: Cambridge University Press, 2006), Todd's recent reference guide is a wonderful beginners guide to Austen. Particularly fine here is Todd's chapters on "Life and Times" and "The Literary Context." I drew on these for coverage of similar material.

Language, Style, and Form

Austen, Jane, *Emma*, ed. James Kinsley (Oxford: Oxford Classics, 2003).

Booth, Wayne, "Control of Distance in Jane Austen's *Emma*," in *The Rhetoric of Fiction* (Chicago: University of Chicago Press, 1961: pp. 243–66). This discussion of *Emma*'s language, style, and form is essential reading to help articulate the ways in which Austen uses free indirect discourse and other ways of controlling the reader's relationship to her characters. According to Booth, Jane Austen's problem in *Emma* is to have the reader reprobate Emma's faults and yet wish for her reform. The solution lies partly in the author's "decision to use Emma's mind as a reflector of events," and thereby lead the reader to hope for her good fortune. But our judgments do not rely solely on Emma. Mr. Knightley provides one corrective, and often the narrator guides the reader directly. Thus, for Booth, Jane Austen achieves a perfect balance of involvement and disinterestedness.

Finch, Casey, and Peter Bowen, "'The Tittle-Tattle of Highbury': Gossip and the Free Indirect Style in *Emma*," *Representations* 31 (1990): pp. 1–18. Argues that in *Emma* both gossip and free indirect discourse act as forms of surveillance, as dispersed, not concentrated, forms of authority, which simultaneously reveal and constitute "the subject as a function of public pressures" and "the community as an extension of the private, individual character." Ultimately enacting "a near epistemological hegemony," the novel completely aligns "the truth of the invisible narrator (located literally nowhere) and the truth of Highbury gossip (located absolutely everywhere)."

Harvey, W. J., "The Plot of *Emma*," in *Essays in Criticism* 17 (1967): pp. 48–63. Harvey's essay is an attempt to counter Wayne Booth's emphasis in *The Rhetoric of Fiction*. If Booth emphasizes the problematic nature of mystery in *Emma*, for Harvey, the idea that the novel's irony depends on solving its mysteries—specifically the secret engagement between Frank Churchill and Jane Fairfax—is wide of the mark. Instead, Harvey argues that the withheld narrative is actually necessary to maintain focus on Emma and to subdue "an otherwise oppressive and facile irony." Far more interesting, according to Harvey's reading, is the binary structure of the plot, and the central narrative's "unwritten twin whose shape is known only by the shadow it casts."

Mudrick, Marvin, *Jane Austen: Irony as Defense and Discovery* (Princeton: Princeton University Press, 1952). Mudrick argues that early in Austen's writing career, in the *Juvenilia*, she adopted irony (consisting "in the discrimination between impulse and pretension, between being and seeming") as her characteristic defense against commitment and feeling. *Emma* represents, for Mudrick, the perfection of Austen's art and her artistic self defense. With *Emma*, Austen attains assured mastery of her technique, "without intrusion of derivativeness or fatigue or morality." For Mudrick, *Emma* appears light but is dense, shaped by interlocking and internal ironic reverberations. The chief irony involves an individual's superficial attractiveness, which signals a separation of wit from feeling. The heroine, probably unrepentant at the end, manipulates people in order to avoid human commitment.

Page, Norman, *The Language of Jane Austen* (New York: Barnes and Noble, 1972). Argues that Austen's style and language are at once traditional and innovative. Austen varies her style from the highly patterned to the flexible and open ended, takes language as a subject for her work, generally resists linguistic change, individualizes dialogue, and explores different ways to render speech. Page's study is still a classic.

Sutherland, John, "Apple-Blossom in June?" in *Is Heathcliff a Murderer?* (New York: Oxford University Press, 1996: pp. 14–19). The book is part of a popular series Sutherland has produced as companions to the Oxford World's Classics series that also includes *Can Jane Eyre Be Happy?* (1997) and *Who Betrays Elizabeth Bennet?* (1999). In these immensely pleasurable encounters with classic literary texts, Sutherland explores narrative inconsistencies and surprising literary and historical allusions. Each short essay is a spin-off of Sutherland's sleuthing as an annotator of fiction. In a time when literary studies have moved steadily and sometimes remorselessly into a world of hyper-serious commitment to theory and ideological critique, Sutherland's essays provide a refreshing respite. They remind us that reading, particularly careful reading, offers pleasure as well as the opportunity to put literature to the service of social and political critique. Sutherland's approach and humor inspire the many closer readings that comprise Austen's *Emma*.

Reading: Themes

Games and Puzzles

Davis, J. M. Q, "*Emma* as Charade and the Education of the Reader," *Philological Quarterly* 65 (1986): pp. 231–42. Contends that although Jane Austen conceives of life as more complex than any conundrum, she yet realizes that "the same principles of reasoning and judgment based on attention to the sober facts are involved in understanding both." She thus has *Emma* overall occupy the same relation to its readers as the novel's games, riddles, and charades do its characters, aiming thereby to wean simultaneously her readers and heroine from identical errors.

Frye, Northrop, *Spiritus Mundi*, (Bloomington: Indiana University Press, 1976). Drawing on the work of sociologist Johan Huizinga, Frye provides a useful Structuralist map for genres such as charm and riddle. Frye's classic study is still essential to the understanding of conventional myths and metaphors and the way they help create archetypes and the generic formulas of classic literature.

Holly, Grant, "*Emma*grammatology," *Studies in Eighteenth-Century Culture* 19, ed. Leslie Ellen Brown and Patricia Craddock (East Lansing, Michigan: Colleagues Press for the American Society for Eighteenth-Century Studies, 1989: pp. 39–52). Not for the faint of heart. Holly's essay draws on Jacques Derrida's *Of Grammatology* (1974) by arguing that *Emma* relentlessly engenders "the play and difference that undermine closure." Underwritten "by the anagrammatic possibilities of misreading and rereading," the novel uses inexactitude, vagueness, and substitutability to regulate "the deployment of character and characteristics" and follows a "pattern of slippage and displacement" to energize "the narrative on the level of the signifier . . . The play of the letter" remains basic to the work, though "anathema to the patriarchal order which sees the floating letter as a sign of castration."

Hecimovich, Gregg, *Puzzling the Reader: Riddles in Nineteenth Century British Literature*, (New York: Peter Lang, 2008). Provides a historical and textual analysis of the role of riddles in nineteenth century British literature, with special attention devoted to Blake, Keats, and Dickens. Includes a theoretical epilogue exploring the riddle's relationship to the theoretical school of deconstruction and the continental philosophy of Martin Heidegger.

Wiesenfarth, Joseph, *Gothic Manners and the Classic English Novel* (Madison: University of Wisconsin Press, 1988). His overarching argument is that the salient elements of two genres, that of the novel of manners and the new Gothic novel, come together and form a synthesis which accounts, in good part, for the greatness of "classical" English fictions. Building upon Bakhtinian premises, and combining scrupulous readings of the texts, Wiesenfarth provides a balanced blend of theory, history, and interpretation to generate an important and useful history of the novel. Of particular note is his examination of the opposing categories of case/riddle in which he associates the case with the novel of manners and the riddle with the Gothic tradition.

Courtship

Huizinga, Johan, *Homo Ludens: A Study of the Play-element in Culture* (Boston: Beacon Press, 1950). Huizinga's groundbreaking book in the field of sociology has proven a touchstone for the literary study of word games. Northrop Frye's *Spiritus Mundi* owes a major debt to Huizinga. Huizinga argues for the need of humans to emerge from *homo sapiens* into *homo ludens*—from "man as knower" into "man the player."

Jolles, Andres, *Einfache Formen*, Translated as *Forms Simples* by Andre Marie Buguet. (Paris: Seuil, 1972) Jolles work helps to establish the opposing categories of the case and the riddle, developed further and applied to English literature by Joseph Wiesenfarth in *Gothic Manners and the Classic English Novel* (1988).

Magee, William, "The Happy Marriage: The Influence of Charlotte Smith on Jane Austen," *Studies in the Novel* 7 (1975): pp. 120–32. Though they differ as regards style, subtlety, and realistic presentation of emotional conflict, Charlotte Smith nevertheless influenced Jane Austen from the beginning to the end of her career, both specifically "in incidental phrasing and situations," and generally, in the theme of courtship and marriage.

Said, Edward, *Beginnings: Intention and Method* (New York: Basic Books, 1975). Traces the ramifications and diverse understandings of the concept of "beginning" (as distinct from "origin") in history. For Said, a "beginning" is its own method, a first step in the intentional production of meaning and the production of difference from pre-existing traditions; as such, a "beginning" authorizes subsequent texts enabling them, while also limiting what becomes acceptable. An "origin" differs; "origins" are divine, mythical, and privileged. Said recognizes in the novel a "beginning," a wide-ranging attempt in Western literary culture to authorize new knowledge from experience. Riddles become interesting in this light because they are associated with both "origins" and "beginnings."

White, Hayden, "The Value of Narrativity in the Representation of Reality," *Critical Inquiry* 7 (1980): pp. 5–27. This article is a concise consolidation of White's influential study *Metahistory* (1973), where White begins his career-long deconstruction of history as narratology controlled by the use of tropes and metaphor.

Conduct

Armstrong, Nancy, *Desire and Domestic Fiction: A Political History of the Novel* (New York: Oxford University Press, 1987). By identifying conduct literature as an important context for Austen's moral outlook, Armstrong exposes the construction of the "domestic woman." The increase in conduct literature in the mid-eighteenth century, which reflected both the rising middle class of women readers and improvements in printing and book distribution, meant that by the time Austen began to write, a new ideal of domesticity had become firmly entrenched in British culture. Like Frances Burney, Austen could, according to Armstrong's reading, "leave the rest of the world alone and deal only with matters of courtship and marriage," but in doing so, her writing was contributing to the regulation of social interaction between classes and sexes. *Emma* is the novel identified by Armstrong as paradigmatic of Austen's special awareness of the power of language to influence human behavior because of its preoccupation with misreading and its challenge to male definitions of social status.

Gilbert, Susan, and Sandra Gubar, *The Madwoman in the Attic: The Woman Writer and the Nineteenth-Century Literary Imagination* (New Haven: Yale University Press, 1979). Gilbert and Gubar revive the late nineteenth-century image of Austen as a spinster lady, to expose the limitations of her domestic circumstances and their regrettable effects on Austen's works. For Gilbert and Gubar, Austen's exuberant creativity, which shines so unmanageably in the early, unpublished writing, was cut and polished to produce acceptable novels for middle class ladies, similarly conditioned by contemporary ideals of female submissiveness. In their account of *Emma*, though the character is the center of her novel, she still "has to learn . . . her commonality with Jane Fairfax, her vulnerability as a female." The story of Emma Woodhouse is, in this reading, not a tale of moral reformation depicting the salvation of a wayward heroine, but rather a narrative of subjugation through which lively female intelligence is forced into "a secondary role of service and silence." Their argument is groundbreaking for its denial of the common reading that takes the novel as a progress: Emma's humiliation, enlightenment, and happy reinstatement in society. Instead, Austen and Emma are silenced by the controlling forces of their society.

Gisborne, Thomas, *An Enquiry into the Duties of the Female Sex* (London: Cadell and Davis, 1797). Argues that women's subordinate nature is innate. While he shares the view that women should not conceal their intellectual abilities, and that parents should never force their daughters into marriage, he commends the traditional feminine virtues and the domestic role for women. Law, politics and government, scholarship, philosophy, navigation and war all "demand the efforts of a mind endued with the powers of close and comprehensive reasoning, and of intense and continued application" and are thus best left to men.

Johnson, Claudia, *Jane Austen: Women, Politics, and the Novel* (Chicago: University of Chicago Press, 1988). Contrary to those who see Jane Austen as conservative, Johnson finds a sophisticated feminist by regarding Austen's work against a neglected tradition of feminine political writing. Though *Emma* fundamentally accepts English class arrangements, the novel also recognizes female rule as positive, featuring a protagonist who disturbs some critics because "she is a woman who possesses and enjoys power, without bother to demur about it." Jane Austen here pictures Emma making legitimate use of her social position and celebrates the "female writing and reading" of others, as well as shows the interpenetration of reality and romance and the dangers of woman's condition. Considered one of the finest studies on Austen in the late twentieth century, Johnson's book is a must read.

Litvak, Joseph, "Reading Characters: Self, Society, and Text in *Emma*," *PMLA* 100 (1985): pp. 763–73. For Litvak, the traditional "Knightleyan" virtues of "strength of mind," "steadiness," "openness," and above all, "reading" are modes of surveillance through which masculine power seeks to exercise control, while Emma's fluidity, fiction-making, and love of riddles are signs of her subversive escape from any fixed, and so controllable, identity. Instead of seeing *Emma* as the tale of a flawed heroine redeemed by good sense, Litvak focuses on the novel's wordplay and evasiveness, arguing not for a straightforward linear plot and denouement but rather for a "potentially endless circuit of fiction, interpretation and desire."

Looser, Devoney, "The Duty of Woman by Woman": Reforming Feminism in *Emma*, in *Emma*, ed. Alistair Duckworth (Boston: Bedford/St. Martin's Press, 2002: pp. 577–93). One of the finest feminist readings of *Emma* in print. Looser places *Emma* into context within conduct literature of the day.

More, Hannah, *Coelebs in Search of a Wife* (London: Cadell and Davis, 1808). A didactic novel in which More uses a young man's search for a wife to present moral teachings in the form of a travel-adventure. By combining conduct literature with evangelical literature, More found popular success with her novel.

Morgan, Susan, *In the Meantime: Character and Perception in Jane Austen's Fiction* (Chicago: University of Chicago Press, 1980). For Morgan, *Emma* "is about the powers of the individual mind, the powers of sympathy and imagination, and about how these powers can find their proper objects in the world outside the mind." When Emma recognizes her own limits and the separate existence of others, life—partly represented by Jane Fairfax, who remains of great value though mysterious and beyond Emma's control—becomes more interesting, the real world larger, and love possible.

Monaghan, David, *Jane Austen: Structure and Social Vision* (Totowa, New Jersey: Barnes and Noble, 1980). Contends that Emma acts humanely toward natives of Highbury, but disregards the feelings of those she considers outsiders. Such inconsistency imposes limits on her development and keeps her world static. Following the expedition to Box Hill, though, where she learns she cannot compartmentalize her world, she begins to treat all people responsibly and "to seek stimulation in a generous engagement with the familiar and in a readiness to accept change."

Nardin, Jane, "Charity in *Emma*," *Studies in the Novel* 7 (1975): pp. 61–72. Treats the theme of charity in *Emma* by noting the ways in which Austen distinguishes "acts in which the donor shows complete respect for the recipient's human dignity and autonomy" from those devoid of such respect. Although Emma begins by assuming, like Mrs. Elton, "that social superiority necessarily implies intellectual and moral superiority," she grows to resemble Mr. Knightley, whose "unobtrusive charity springs naturally from close daily contract and formal visits of investigation and aid."

Sulloway, Alison, *Jane Austen and the Province of Womanhood* (Philadelphia: University of Pennsylvania Press, 1989) Argues that eighteenth-century attitudes to "the woman question," ranging from conservative and patriarchal to moderately feminist to radical, helped shape Austen's novels, providing her with models of both women's evolutionary and revolutionary development. Those defending the status quo, including male writers of conduct books and periodical essayists, dismissed women's dignity and desire for autonomy, arguing for men's rightful "pride in their dominion and their prejudice against the sex they dominated through their presumed superiority." Sulloway's book provides an excellent survey of conduct literature and its influence on Austen.

Weber, Harold, *The Restoration Rake-Hero* (Madison: University of Wisconsin Press, 1986). Charts the development of the rake figure from the sixteenth to the eighteenth centuries against changing sexual attitudes. Weber holds that scholars have underestimated the power of the rake figure in shaping narrative well into the early nineteenth century.

Wellbeing

Gorman, Anita, *The Body in Illness and Health: Themes and Images in Jane Austen* (New York: Peter Lang, 1993). Contends that Austen's novels reflect her culture's "medical preoccupations" by using health, and actual and imagined illness, to advance plot, define character, and present such themes as self-knowledge and growth. For Gorman, Austen recognizes life's frailty, and endorses vitality and beauty when they combine with benevolence rather than self-centeredness, believing both that the body can cure itself and that the mind can either weaken or cure the body.

Heydt-Stevenson, Jill, "'Slipping into the Ha-Ha': Bawdy Humor and Body Politics in Jane Austen's Novels," *Nineteenth-Century Literature* 55 (2000): pp. 309–39. Contends that the novels of Jane Austen are filled with instances of sexually risqué humor, but that this aspect of her comedy has rarely been recognized or subjected to extended critical comment and analysis. This essay examines the way in which Austen integrates bawdy humor into *Emma*, *Mansfield Park*, and *Persuasion* in the service of critiquing patriarchal culture and as a way to affirm the vigorous reality of female sexuality.

Miller, D. A., "The Late Jane Austen," Raritan 10 (1990): pp. 55–79. Argues that in Austen's six major novels "health either goes without saying as the necessary condition of the socially productive, reproductive body, or only speaks to utter the discourse of hypochondria, which in turn gets ironized into reinforcing the socio-moral code." Emma proves a late example of Miller's contention. But in *Sanditon*, hypochondria no longer opposes the social but itself becomes sociable: a "morbidity culture" emerges, one linked to economic incentives and warranting the disintegration of Austen's typical marriage plot.

Preus, Nicholas, "Sexuality in *Emma*: A Case History," *Studies in the Novel* 23 (1991): pp. 196–216. Contends that in *Emma* Austen encodes "the secret that is not a secret"—sexuality—in the novel's conundrums, "cultural semiotics," and chronology, presenting "three cases of sexuality" and linking each "to social and even biological truth systems." Writing at a time of historical transition regarding "kinship relations" and the norms of marriage, Austen reveals that sex constitutes the self's truth while mutuality (tolerance, intelligence, and good will) constitutes society's truth.

Sales, Roger, *Jane Austen and Representations of Regency England* (New York: Routledge, 1994). Sales provides an encyclopedic exploration of the Regency context for Austen's novels. The chapter on *Emma* draws fascinating parallels between the Apothecaries' Act of 1815 and the novel, written around the same time. For Sales, *Emma* connects sickness with leisure and mobility with power and opposes the village and the watering place, professionalism and idleness, English and French attitudes. Austen's *Emma* does not, ultimately, resolve the complexities it explores; instead, though committed to an ethic of work, it also finds worth in the "secrets and mysteries" of the disruptive Frank Churchill.

Watson, J. R., "Mr Perry's Patients: A View of *Emma*," *Essays in Criticism* 20 (1970): pp. 334–43. One of the first critical studies to discuss health as a theme in *Emma*. Argues that in *Emma* "the comedy about health is able to illuminate character in a significant way." By its combination of the serious and the amusing, the health theme fulfills the ethical potential of comedy.

Wiltshire, John, *Jane Austen and the Body* (Cambridge: Cambridge University Press, 1992). In Wiltshire's groundbreaking study, he enquires into the part that health—whether moral, spiritual, psychological, or physical—plays in Austen's novels, using contemporary eighteenth-century medical treatises to indicate the background against which the works were composed. The chapter on *Emma* examines "spirits" and "nerves." One of the best books written on Austen, and on *Emma*!

CRITICAL RECEPTION AND PUBLISHING HISTORY

Austen, Jane, "Opinions of *Emma*," in *Minor Works*, volume 6 of *The Novels of Jane Austen*, ed. R. W. Chapman (Oxford: Oxford University Press, 1952).

Austen-Leigh, James, *A Memoir of Jane Austen*, 1870, ed. Kathryn Sutherland (Oxford: Oxford University Press, 2002).

Brontë, Charlotte, *The Letters of Charlotte Brontë*, ed. Margaret Smith, 3 volumes (Oxford: Clarendon Press, 1995–2004)

Butler, Marilyn, *Maria Edgeworth: A Literary Biography* (Oxford: Clarendon Press, 1972). Austen admired much about Edgeworth's fiction and styled herself in some fashion after Edgeworth. Butler's important biography is useful for drawing a deeper understanding of Austen as well as Edgeworth.

DiPaolo, Marc, *Emma Adapted: Jane Austen's Heroine from Book to Film* (New York: Peter Lang, 2007).

Duckworth, Alistair, "A Critical History of *Emma*," in *Emma*, ed. Alistair Duckworth (New York: Palgrave, 2002: 405–24). An excellent and thorough survey of *Emma*'s critical reception. *Austen's "Emma"* draws heavily on this work and Fiona Stafford's "Introduction," cited below.

Fergus, Jan, "The Professional Woman Writer," in *The Cambridge Companion to Jane Austen*, ed. Edward Copeland and Juliet McMasters (Cambridge: Cambridge University Press, 1997: pp. 12–31)

Halperin, John, "Jane Austen's Nineteenth-Century Critics: Walter Scott to Henry James," in *Jane Austen: Bicentenary Essays*, ed. John Halperin (New York: Cambridge University Press, 1975). An excellent collection of hard-to-gather nineteenth-century responses to Austen.

Johnson, Claudia, "Austen Cults and Cultures," in *The Cambridge Companion to Jane Austen*, ed. Edward Copeland and Juliet McMasters (Cambridge: Cambridge University Press, 1997: pp. 211–26)

Jones, M. G., *Hannah More* (New York: Greenwood, 1968).

Kohn, Denise, "Reading *Emma* as a Lesson on 'Ladyhood': A Study in the Domestic Bildungsroman," *Essays in Literature* 22 (1995): pp. 45–58. Argues that *Emma* is an example of a Bildungsroman in which a heroine's education and development as a lady is achieved in a domestic setting rather than through a quest: "[H]eroines such as Emma do have to overcome obstacles in order to become adult, and these obstacles are often domesticated or different versions of those that heroes face on their quest for independence."

Lawrence, D. H., "A Propos of *Lady Chatterley's Lover*," in *Lady Chatterley's Lover*, ed. Michael Squires, *The Cambridge Edition of the Works of D. H. Lawrence* (Cambridge: Cambridge University Press, 1993).

Leavis, F. R., *The Great Tradition* (London: Chatto, 1948).

Lewes, G. H. "The Novels of Jane Austen," *Blackwood's Edinburgh Magazine* (July 1859): pp. 99–113.

Litz, A. Walton, *Jane Austen: A Study of Her Artistic Development* (New York: Oxford University Press, 1965). A great starting point for exploring modern interpretations of *Emma*. For Litz, Austen's novel values equally imagination and reason; fulfillment is realized through total self-knowledge. By accepting Mr. Knightley, Emma unites common sense with imaginative perception and the real with the ideal. In allowing the reader to share Emma's inner life without being limited by it, Austen overcomes a problem of the earlier novels: she avoids the dichotomy between sympathetic imagination and critical judgment.

Mukherjee, Meenakshi, *Women Writers: Jane Austen* (New York: St. Martin's Press, 1991). Mukherjee argues for a feminist Austen who struggles to enact her feminism within the realistic confines of her novels. The novels, which mediate ironically between historical reality and available literary rhetoric, mirror Austen's uneasy, double-edged attitude to marriage. Thus, though a heroine like Emma achieves relative equality with her husband, less important couples in the works testify mostly to conjugal failure, leaving Austen to close her novels in a hasty, indirect manner, with "an embarrassed avoidance of detail."

Scott, Walter, *The Journal of Sir Walter Scott* [From the Original Manuscript at Abbotsford] (1890)

Schorer, Mark, "The Humiliation of Emma Woodhouse," in *Jane Austen: A Collection of Critical Essays*, ed. Ian Watt (Englewood Cliffs: Prentice Hall, 1963: pp. 98–111). Argues that *Emma* employs a style whose metaphors derive from "commerce and property," immersing the reader into a "world of peculiarly *material* value." Her comedy arises from the juxtaposition of this world with that of ostensible or real moral propriety. *Emma*'s structure reflects Austen's double intention of verifying the values of her society and of judging them. Thus, "as the heroine comes into partial self-recognition . . . at the same time [she] sinks more completely into that society."

Southam, B. C., ed. *Jane Austen: The Critical Heritage* (New York: Barnes and Noble, 1968)

Southam, B. C., ed. *Jane Austen: The Critical Heritage: Volume 2, 1870–1940* (New York: Routledge, 1987)

Stafford, Fiona, "Introduction," in *Jane Austen's Emma: A Casebook*, ed. Fiona Stafford (Oxford: Oxford University Press, 2007): pp. 1–35. A concise and comprehensive survey of *Emma*'s critical reception to the present day. *Austen's "Emma"* draws heavily on this work.

Tobin, Beth, "Aiding Impoverished Gentlewomen: Power and Class in *Emma*," *Criticism* 30 (1998): pp. 413–31. Contends that Emma's snobbery is a function of her vanity, and her fear of other, less socially important women than herself, whose real virtues and beauty would outshine hers if they occupied the same privileged position in society. According to Tobin, Emma fails to grow as a heroine because of her fatal snobbishness and elitism.

Todd, Janet, "Social Friendship," in *Women's Friendship in Literature* (New York: Columbia, 1980: pp. 246–301). Argues that Emma seeks to define women's social friendship, "picturing its abuse as well as its use, admitting its necessary limits in an ordinary world of marriage and subordinate women, and indicating its potential to help a young girl discover herself and a world beyond the family." Although Emma properly outgrows Mrs. Weston and Harriet, she never really establishes a satisfying relationship with her equal, Jane Fairfax.

Watt, Ian, *The Rise of the Novel: Studies in Defoe, Richardson, and Fielding* (London: Chatto, 1957).

ADAPTATION AND INTERPRETATION

Television and/or film adaptations: books and essays

Blum, Virginia, "The Return to Repression: Filming the Nineteenth Century," in *Jane Austen and Co.*, ed. Suzanne R. Pucci and James Thompson (Albany: State University of New York Press, 2003).

Boose, Lynda E. and Richard Burt, "Totally *Clueless*? Shakespeare Goes Hollywood in the 1990s," in *Film and Literature*, ed. Timothy Corrigan (New Jersey: Prentice Hall, 1998).

Corrigan, Timothy, ed. *Film and Literature* (Upper Saddle River, NJ: Prentice-Hall, 1999).

DiPaolo, Marc, *Emma Adapted: Jane Austen's Heroine from Book to Film* (New York: Peter Lang, 2007).

Harris, Jocelyn, "A Review of Three Austen Adaptations," *Eighteenth Century Fiction* 8 (1996): p. 430.

Lauritzen, Laurie, *Jane Austen's Emma on Television: A Study of a BBC Classic Serial.* (Sweden: Minab, 1981).

Lynch, Deidre, "*Clueless* About History," in *Jane Austen and Co.*, ed. Suzanne R. Pucci and James Thompson (Albany: State University of New York Press, 2003), pp. 71–92.

Mazmanian, Melissa, "Reviving *Emma* in a *Clueless* World: The Current Attraction to a Classic Structure," *Persuasions: The Jane Austen Journal On-line*, Occasional Papers No. 3, 1999, http://www.jasna.org/persuasions/on-line/opno3/mazmanian.html.

Monaghan, David, "Emma and the Art of Adaptation," in *Jane Austen on Screen*, ed. Gina Macdonald and Andrew Macdonald (Cambridge: Cambridge University Press, 2003), pp. 197–227.

Morrison, Sarah, "*Emma* Minus Its Narrator: Decorum and Class Consciousness in Film Versions of the Novel," *Persuasions: The Jane Austen Journal On-line*, Occasional Papers No. 3, 1999, http://www.jasna.org/persuasions/on-line/opno3/morrison.html.

Mosier, John, "Clues for the *Clueless*," in *Jane Austen on Screen*, ed. Gina Macdonald and Andrew Macdonald (Cambridge: Cambridge University Press, 2003), pp. 228–53).

Nachumi, Nora, "'As If!': Translating Austen's Ironic Narrator to Film," *in Jane Austen in Hollywood*, ed Linda Troost and Sayrre Greenfield (Lexington: University Press of Kentucky, 1998), pp. 130–39.

Palmer, Sally, "Robbing the Roost: Reinventing Socialism in Diarmuid Lawrence's *Emma*," *Persuasions: The Jane Austen Journal On-line*,

Occasional Papers No. 3, 1999, http://www.jasna.org/persuasions/on-line/opno3/palmer.html.

Parrill, Sue, "The Cassandra of Highbury: Miss Bates on Film," *Persuasions: The Jane Austen Journal On-line*, Occasional Papers No. 3, 1999, http://www.jasna.org/persuasions/on-line/opno3/parrill.html.

Parrill, Sue, *Jane Austen on Film and Television: A Critical Study of the Adaptations* (London: McFarland and Company, 2002).

Parrill, Sue, "Metaphors of Control: Physicality in *Emma* and *Clueless*," *Persuasions: The Jane Austen Journal On-line* Volume 20, Number 1, http://www.jasna.org/persuasions/on-line/vol20no1/parrill.html.

Restuccia, Frances, "A Black Morning: Kristevan Melancholia in Jane Austen's *Emma*," *American Imago: Studies in Psychoanalysis and Culture* 51 (1994): pp. 447–69.

Schor, Hilary, "Emma, Interrupted: Speaking Jane Austen in Fiction and Film," in *Jane Austen on Screen*, ed. Gina Macdonald and Andrew Macdonald (Cambridge: Cambridge University Press, 2003), pp. 144–74.

Thompson, James, "How to Do Things with Austen," in *Jane Austen and Co.*, ed. Suzanne R. Pucci and James Thompson (Albany: State University of New York Press, 2003), pp. 13–32.

Troost, Linda, and Sayre Greenfield, "Filming Highbury: Reducing the Community in *Emma* to the Screen," *Persuasions: The Jane Austen Journal On-line*, Occasional Papers No. 3, 1999, http://www.jasna.org/persuasions/on-line/opno3/troost_sayre.html.

Troost, Linda, ed. *Jane Austen in Hollywood* (Lexington: University Press of Kentucky, 1998).

Turim, Maureen, "Popular Culture and the Comedy of Manners: *Clueless* and Fashion Clues," in *Jane Austen and Co.*, ed. Suzanne R. Pucci and James Thompson (Albany: State University of New York Press, 2003), pp. 13–32.

Wald, Gayle, "*Clueless* in the Neo-Colonial World Order," *The Postmodern Jane Austen*, ed. You-me Park and Rajeswari Sunder Rajan (New York: Routledge, 2000), pp. 218–33.

DVDs

DVDs of the Douglas McGrath 1996 film *Emma*, the Andrew Davies–Diarmuid Lawrence 1996 film *Jane Austen's 'Emma'*, and Amy Heckerling's 1995 film *Clueless* are widely available. The 1972 "Glenister-Constanduros" version is available from Netflix.com.

INDEX